PREACHING CHRIST TODAY

Preaching Christ Today

The Gospel and Scientific Thinking

THOMAS F. TORRANCE

WILLIAM B. EERDMANS PUBLISHING COMPANY
GRAND RAPIDS, MICHIGAN

Printed in the United States of America

00 99 98 97 96 95 94   7 6 5 4 3 2 1

Library of Congress Cataloging-in-Publication Data

Torrance, Thomas Forsyth, 1913-
Preaching Christ today: The Gospel and
Scientific Thinking / Thomas F. Torrance.
        p.   cm.
ISBN 0-8028-0799-2
1. Bible and science. 2. Evangelistic work. 3. Incarnation.
4. Atonement. I. Title.
BS650.T67   1994
251 — dc20   94-35032
                                    CIP

Contents

To

Billy Graham

*in gratitude for his
proclamation of the gospel
in Scotland*

Preface

L ong ago my old teacher, Professor Hugh Ross Mackintosh of New
College, Edinburgh, published a small booklet entitled "The Heart of
the Gospel and the Preacher," in which he advocated doctrinal preaching
of the gospel centered on the atonement. He recalled how the greatest
preachers of the past were also great teachers of doctrine, and he pointed
out that it was in the combination of preaching and doctrine that the very
heart of the gospel was brought to bear with power upon people in
English-speaking lands. He instanced the preaching of Newman and Dale
in England and Bushnell and Brooks in America, but I would point
particularly to Mackintosh himself, who as a great teacher of Christian
doctrine was also a rare preacher of the gospel.

I refer here to Mackintosh since it was under his influence that
some of us founded the Scottish Church Theology Society dedicated
to the renewal of theology in the teaching and preaching of the church
in Scotland. That is the end to which my own life has been dedicated.
What I have been trying to do is to show how the gospel can be taught
and preached in ways that are faithful to the apostolic faith as it was
brought to authoritative expression in the Nicene Creed, and at the
same time may be taught and preached today in ways that can be
expressed and appreciated within the scientific understanding of the
created universe upon which God has impressed his Word and which
under God we have been able to develop in modern times. Far from
being hostile to one another, Christian theology and natural science

are complementary to one another. I believe that science owes much more to the Christian faith than is usually recognized, and that science may be harnessed in the service of the gospel which humankind so desperately needs today.

The two addresses that make up this booklet are meant primarily for ministers of the gospel and for theological students preparing for the ministry of the gospel.

The first of these addresses was delivered on the occasion of the Jubilee of the Scottish Church Theology Society, recalling its formal inauguration at the General Assembly of the Church of Scotland in 1943. It is a plea to return to Christ-centered teaching and preaching, to theological evangelism. In it I call for renewed appreciation of the way in which in the New Testament preaching and teaching are inseparably intertwined. I have tried to show how a faithful scientific approach to biblical interpretation does not detract from this but deepens it, in such a way that the evangelical and doctrinal presentation of the gospel of the incarnate, crucified, and risen Savior can be released today in its true force.

The second address was delivered to the Theological Students' Forum of Princeton Theological Seminary. Over the years I have been a frequent visitor to Princeton, not least in connection with my work at the Center of Theological Inquiry, which was established there to cultivate a theological renaissance through research at the open face of advance in fundamental knowledge of God and the world, in which knowledge of God and of the created universe are linked together at points of their deepest convergence. I believe that as we examine the profound conceptual interrelations between theology and science, our understanding of Christian doctrine and our preaching of the gospel, grounded upon the incarnation and the atonement, will be able to match the spiritual and intellectual needs of the hour.

Edinburgh
Advent, 1993

Preaching Christ Today

Preaching Christ is both an evangelical and a theological activity, for it is the proclamation and teaching of Christ as he is actually presented to us in the Holy Scriptures. In the language of the New Testament, preaching Christ involves *kerygma* and *didache* — it is both a *kerygmatic* and a *didactic* activity. It is both *evangelical* and *theological*. This is a feature in the Gospels to which my former colleague in New College, James S. Stewart, more than any other New Testament scholar known to me, sought to be faithful in his lectures, which he delivered in a kerygmatic and a didactic mode. He interpreted the text of the Gospels and expounded the gospel in the Gospels in such a way that his students heard the living and dynamic Word of God for themselves. Not surprisingly many of them were converted in his classroom. No wonder that Jim Stewart was such a beloved preacher and teacher of gospel truth. It was James Denney who used to say that our theologians should be evangelists and our evangelists theologians. This is something, I believe, we must learn again in our calling to preach Christ today.

I

The first thing I want to talk about in preaching Christ is the interrelation between *kerygma* and *didache*. The church's calling is to proclaim Christ kerygmatically and didactically — we need didactic preaching, and kerygmatic theology. The only Christ there was and is, as John Calvin used to say, is not a naked Christ but "Christ clothed with his gospel." By that he meant that Jesus Christ and his Word, Jesus Christ and the truth of his message belong inseparably together and may not be torn apart. With us human beings person, word, and act are separate, but this is not the case with Jesus, the Word made flesh, full of grace and truth, for in him person, word, and act are one. That is why when we read and interpret the Gospels and Epistles and let them talk to us out of themselves we find ourselves having to do directly with God in Christ "speaking to us in person," as Athanasius and Calvin both used to say.

Unfortunately this is the very thing that some New Testament scholarship today does not seem to promote in its so-called quest for the historical Jesus. I think here of one of the most radical New Testament scholars of our times, Rudolf Bultmann of Marburg. He did his best to "demythologize" Jesus, or strip away from the New Testament "Jesus" the theological frame in which he is presented to us by the evangelists and apostles, on the ground that the didactic or theological material derives not from the historical Jesus but from the early Christian community. But you cannot stop there in peeling away layers of so-called theological interpretation put upon Christ. I recall how one of the professors in my old university in Basel, Fritz Buri, attempted to do just that, and set himself to strip away from Jesus not only the didactic material in the Gospels but the *kerygma* as well, and so to detach the historical event of Jesus completely from his evangelical message. He decided to give three public lectures on *Entkerugmatisierung*, or the *dekerygmatizing* of the gospel, thereby going beyond Bultmann's demythologizing program in seeking to strip Jesus naked of his gospel. Karl Barth decided to go along and listen to these lectures. Later when he met Fritz Buri in the street he said to him with his customary humor: "Now at last, brother Buri, I know the difference between you and Bultmann. When Bultmann goes in for a swim he at least has a pair of bathing trunks on!"

When you begin to tear these elements in the Holy Scriptures apart, the kerygmatic from the didactic, the historical from the theological, everything goes wrong. Is this not what New Testament scholarship so often does today in its adherence to what it calls "the historical scientific method," and thereby undermines evangelical and theological preaching?

I was particularly intrigued once in coming across a similar problem in the researches of the social anthropologists, Evans-Pritchard on the Azande culture in Africa, and Clyde Kluckholn on the culture of the Navaho Indians in the southwestern states of America. Let me refer only to the latter. He spent a long time with the Navaho Indians, studying their institutions and patterns of behavior at first hand in direct, carefully and meticulously controlled observations of their way of life, but after many years he realized that he had not really understood them. He had made a point of being as scientifically accurate and objective as possible in establishing the empirical data, but the Navahos would not accept his results. The trouble was that he had been interpreting and integrating what he observed with a conceptual frame of thought alien to the Navahos. Then when he set himself to study the institutions and behavior of the Navahos again through living with them and absorbing their way of thinking in describing and integrating their own way of life, he found that what he now wrote up about them not only made sense to the Navahos but made scientific sense as well, for this way of conceptualizing what he observed from the inside, as it were, made his observations and judgments accurate and objective in a way that they had not been before.

Learning from Inverting Spectacles

Let me show you what has been happening in the analysis of the New Testament texts by reference to the results of a famous experiment with inverting spectacles that has been carried out in different parts of the world, for example at Wichita in Kansas. These are spectacles that make you see things upside down and the wrong way round, so that everything becomes disorderly and chaotic. Your orientation to the world around you is completely upset, so that you stagger about. You can't act in a natural and balanced way in relation to the objective realities around you, chairs, tables, doors, and so on, for you bump into them

3

and stumble around. But after eight painful days you become oriented to the world round you in an orderly way again, and can start moving about without tumbling over the furniture or running into things.

What is happening? When you put on these inverting spectacles you tear the visual image away from the mental image — the perceptual image from the conceptual image — and everything becomes topsy turvy. That is the sort of thing that happens in the kind of New Testament scholarship I have been speaking about when the kerygmatic and didactic elements in the biblical narrative, the empirical and theological factors, are split apart, and their original cohesion is lost.

There is something fundamentally wrong going on here with the so-called historical scientific method, which needs to be carefully understood, for it is terribly important — it has to do with the interrelation of *kerygma* and *didache* and the wholeness of the New Testament witness to Christ. James Stewart was rather hurt when a thesis was published about him, arguing that he didn't appreciate historical scientific method. Actually he knew much better than his critics about the real issues at stake in attempts to interpret the New Testament Scriptures in a way that is both faithful and academic, for he sought to interpret the texts of the New Testament strictly in accordance with what they actually are as they have been handed on to us in the inseparable interrelation of *kerygma* and *didache,* and not in accordance with some analysis and reconstruction imposed upon them *ab extra.* He sought to interpret the apostolic witness to Christ in light of its implicit wholeness in order to let it speak to us as far as possible out of itself.

We must now ask, What is meant by "historical scientific method"?

"Historical" method What kind of *history* is being envisaged? Well, let's think again of Bultmann, held to be one of the great New Testament scholars of our times. He drew a sharp line of distinction between two kinds of history called *Historie* and *Geschichte,* the kind of history that is interpreted in terms of strict causal connections, and the kind of history that is interpreted in terms of how things appear to us. That distinction goes back through Herrmann and Kant to Lessing's "ugly

4

big ditch" between necessary truths of reason and accidental truths of history, but ultimately it derives from the radical dualism between "absolute mathematical time" and "relative apparent time" posited by Newton in his system of the world. That is the dualism that lay at the heart of the determinist conception of the universe, which has played so much havoc with our understanding of nature and its relation to God and ruled out of rational consideration anything that could not be explained in terms of physical laws, so that not a little of our human experience and culture which we cherish and value could be understood and explained only on a subjective basis.

The Newtonian distinction between two kinds of time, along with the mathematical formalization of the laws of motion, was highly abstract and artificial and left no room for "real time," or therefore for salvation history. That is why, of course, Bultmann held that *Historie* understood in this natural causalist way ruled out any thought of incarnation or miracles or resurrection, or of God's interaction with us in history. His acceptance of the idea of an unbroken continuity of cause and effect governed by natural law made him regard the central Christian beliefs embedded in the Gospels and Epistles of the New Testament as a mythological account of reported this-worldly events in other-worldly ways lacking objective truth and reality. They were no more than subjective forms of thought devised by the early church in order to make existential sense of the way Jesus was reported to have appeared to his followers. Hence Bultmann devised a "program of demythologizing" and reinterpreting the New Testament existentially in which modern people can make sense of the New Testament in terms of their own self-understanding in the scientific world of classical Newtonian mechanics.

The Newtonian conception of absolute mathematical time and space clamped down upon the universe, along with its rational dualism between empirical events and theoretical constructions, gave rise to a rigidly mechanistic account of nature which James Clerk Maxwell found could not explain the behavior of light. A new scientific approach to the created universe and a very different understanding of nature in terms of continuous dynamic fields had to be developed. This reconstruction of the foundations of science, which Albert Einstein held to be the most important in history, led him to develop his theories of special and general relativity. They shattered the determinist conceptions of classical mechanics and led to quantum theory, and a much more refined and dynamic and open-ended understanding of reality. We cannot go into that here, but it will be sufficient for our purpose to note that Einstein overthrew the dualist disjunction between empirical events and scientific theory or between physical facts and mathematics. He showed that if scientists are to be true to the nature of the space-time universe, they must not try to interpret it by crushing their understanding of it into a preconceived static frame of ideas formulated altogether apart from the physical structures of nature, as the Newtonians had done with the timeless necessary system of Euclidean geometry. Everything finally goes wrong when that is done. Rather must geometry be put into the heart of physics where it is transformed through being embedded in the dynamic world of space-time and becomes four-dimensional. This means that geometrical patterns and physical structures in our space-time universe are bound inseparably together; conceptual and empirical factors inhere in one another, both in nature and in our understanding of it, and must not be torn apart. That is why our twentieth-century science has made such enormous advance, for it no longer imposes abstract necessary patterns of thought upon nature, but seeks to understand nature out of its own inherent rational order, and is therefore concerned with continuous dynamic fields and with real time.

There we have the immense revolution in the foundations of knowledge brought about through general relativity theory, followed up by quantum theory, which has now been built into rigorous modern science. This involves a way of thinking in which experiment and theory, empirical and theoretical factors interact with one another and must not be divorced from one another, and therefore a way of thinking in which the historical and the conceptual ingredients must be taken together in the understanding of any historical culture or religion. The extraordinary thing is that our biblical scholars seem to show very little knowledge of this revolution and correction in the foundations of rational and scientific knowledge. They still work with a dichotomy between empirical and theoretical factors in knowledge, and with the old discarded notions of split time expressed in their two kinds of history. I don't know any scientist who accepts what biblical scholars say about *Historie* and *Geschichte*. Actually even the German secular historians don't operate with this artificial concept of a twofold history. Quite clearly, biblical scholars need to turn their attention to conceptions of real time and real history if they are to do justice to salvation history and to the intrinsic truth of Christ clothed with his gospel.

"Scientific" method   The kind of scientific method that became dominant after the Enlightenment in the eighteenth century concentrated first upon the isolation and observation of phenomena, and then set about establishing natural laws through logical deduction from the empirical data reached in that way, but that meant, as even Kant admitted, reading laws into nature, not reading them out of nature. This is known as the phenomenalist and constructivist conception of science. Scientific theories were reached through observing and analyzing of phenomena and then imposing upon them the necessitarian framework of absolute mathematical time and space, in order to give the phenomenalist particulars some kind of rational coherence. This is the kind of scientific method which produced the hard determinist conception of the universe that has done so much damage to all areas of human thought.

Think what happens when that kind of scientific method governs research into the culture of the Navaho Indians. First of all you isolate and determine the empirical data and try to describe them in strictly empirical or observationalist terms. When you have done that, you interpret them, not through a conceptuality inherent in them, but through a conceptual frame of thought derived elsewhere, e.g., from a mechanist theory of evolution. As we have noted, that is the kind of scientific method which Clyde Kluckholn found to be disastrously wrong. And that is precisely the false scientific method that has now been comprehensively destroyed in physics, the most rigorous of all sciences, in the rejection of a dualism between empirical and conceptual factors, or between phenomena and theory. Proper scientific method seeks to penetrate into the intrinsic rationality of any field of reality, grasping it in depth, as Einstein argued, in order to understand it in accordance with its distinctive nature, and to find appropriate ways of formulating knowledge of what is learned in this way. That is actually how scientific method normally operates today.

The Loss of Biblical Wholeness

But what have biblical scholars been doing with their so-called historical scientific method? In examining the biblical records they try to determine the truth about the historical Jesus, through giving critical attention to empirical data in isolation from any theological factors. Thus when they come to passages such as we find in Matthew 11 or Luke 10, where Jesus is reported to have said, "No one knows the Son but the Father and no one knows the Father but the Son and he to whom the Son reveals him," they argue that the historical Jesus could not have said that, for in accordance with their preconceptions that must be put down to theological interpretation that came later, from the early church's attempt to understand Jesus. They say the same thing about the command of the risen Jesus to institute baptism in the name of the Father, of the Son, and of the Holy Spirit. Although there is no textual evidence against either passage, they insist that they could not have come originally from Jesus himself! Why? Because, they argue, those reported sayings of Jesus have a theological ingredient which cannot "scientifically" be accepted as part of the empirical data relating to the historical Jesus. Hence, for extraneous dogmatic reasons, they cut out theological elements from the Gospels and attribute them to the activity of the Christian community. Thus these biblical scholars through their historical scientific method tear the empirical and the theoretical, the historical and theological ingredients, apart from one another, thereby doing exactly the same thing that we find happening with inverting spectacles, which disrupt vision by tearing apart the perceptual image from the conceptual image. Hence it is not surprising that New Testament scholarship today is in a rather chaotic state. It is largely due to this analytical approach dismembering the biblical witness that some scholars claim to find several "Christologies" in the New Testament — they cannot see the wood for the trees!

How different was the early account given by St. John in his first Epistle, in which the empirical events of seeing, hearing, and touching Jesus are found interwoven with the gospel message of Christ as the incarnate Son of God who gave himself in sacrifice to be the propitiation for our sins. The real Jesus of history is the Christ who cannot be separated from his saving acts, for his person and his work are one, Christ clothed with his gospel of saving grace. The so-called Jesus of history shorn of theological truth is an abstraction invented by a pseudo-scientific method.

The questionable state of affairs in New Testament scholarship today brought about through the divorce of historical and theological ingredients is such that a few years ago Professor Michael Dummet, the Oxford mathematical philosopher, wrote a couple of articles in the magazine *New Blackfriars* charging New Testament scholars with a "fraudulent" handling of the resurrection narratives in the Gospels. The foundations of New Testament scholarship are now under attack and changes are being made, not least in a reintegration of historical events and divine revelation. This is increasingly evident in the way in which the New Testament documents are being interpreted in relation to a Hebraic, and not a Hellenistic, frame of mind, so that Jesus is being understood again in the light of God's redemptive self-revelation to Israel and indeed not just in the light of the documents of rabbinic Judaism on which some scholars have been concentrating. This is having the effect of stripping away from Jesus the clothes of Gentile culture with which he has been robed and obscured. Another of the significant changes taking place, I am told, is the questioning of the Q Hypothesis, which arose under the analytical activities of the historical scientific method and the kind of reconstruction that had to be attempted after the natural connection of empirical and theological factors was disrupted. When you tear the visual and mental images apart, or sever the connection between the

9

perceptual and conceptual ingredients in knowledge, then some sort of extraneous matter has to be introduced in order to make the dismembered results of this kind of historical critical research stick together. But all the time the real historical Jesus slips through the fingers of those critical New Testament scholars like sand. The historical Jesus and the theological Christ cannot be separated from one another without grave misunderstanding of the gospel and serious detriment to the faith of the church.

The Divorce of Kerygma and Didache

What I am trying to say, then, is that this divorce of the empirical from the theoretical which involves the divorce of *kerygma* from *didache* disrupts and damages the biblical presentation of Jesus Christ in such a way that people find it difficult to preach, for all it offers is a Christ stripped bare of his divine truth. If you cannot preach the gospel didactically as well as kerygmatically, you have to invent your own theology to make these things stick together. But once Humpty-Dumpty has fallen like that, all the king's horses and all the king's men cannot put him together again — that's the problem, and it is a far bigger problem than many people realize.

I have challenged New Testament scholars deliberately about this problem in the introduction and last chapter of my book *Space, Time, and Resurrection,* and I have raised these issues in public lectures in different universities, but not a single New Testament scholar has offered me any answers! I can understand that, because in order to do so they have to rethink their understanding of what took place in the relation between the early church and Hellenistic philosophy and science and to face up to the similar revolution in the foundations of knowledge in our own times, delivering it from the damaging dualisms of the past, which, thank God, has been brought about in our day through modern science, and that may involve some very hard thinking for them.

Let me refer again to James Clerk Maxwell, our great Scottish

10

scientist who began this remarkable clarification in knowledge when he rejected the mechanical model of thought in his dynamical theory of the electromagnetic field. He showed that we cannot think of connections in nature in terms of action at a distance, through the bearing of atoms or particles externally upon one another. Rather must we think in terms of continuous dynamic field structures in which particles are interlocked with one another in a much more profound integrated form of rationality. That is the only way we can think in theology as well, in the light of the intrinsic intelligibility of God's interaction with us in his revealing and saving acts in space and time in history, as indeed Maxwell himself pointed out from his own deeply Christian convictions.

That is the first thing I want to say. I believe this to be terribly important, for to interpret Jesus Christ under the guidance of the kind of rationalist historical scientific method long discarded by science actually destroys a proper understanding of the humanity of Jesus and of the kerygmatic and didactic way in which he confronts us in the Gospels.

II

This brings me to the second thing I want to stress in preaching Christ, the unbroken relation between the sheer humanity of Jesus and God. The New Testament opens with the announcement by the angel of the Lord that the child to be born of Mary was to be called both *Jeshua* (*Jahweh* saves) and *Immanuel* (*God* with us). The Jesus of whom we read in the Gospels and whom we proclaim as Christ is both man of Israel and the Lord God, for in him God himself has come to be with us, really to be with us as one of us and as God for us, who has taken our human nature upon himself, our sin and guilt, our misery and death, in order to save and heal us, and as such really to be our God. How do we put these two facts together, that Jesus Christ is both *man* of Israel and our *God?* Everything in the gospel depends on that twofold truth.

How do you interpret the New Testament if you tear Jesus out of the revelationary context in which he is presented to us and tear apart the empirical and the theological aspects of the gospel with which he is essentially bound up? When you do that, you inevitably interpret Jesus in terms of your own self-understanding and culture in the West or the East and so put an alien Gentile image upon the face of Jesus. When that is done our Jewish brethren cannot recognize their own promised Messiah in our Jesus. But that is not the real Jesus, for Jesus was a Jew. Properly to understand Jesus we must not detach him from the people of Israel but think of him as a Hebrew of the Hebrews who may be understood only out of the midst of God's long interaction with Israel, chosen to be the medium of his self-revelation to humankind. Thank God, as I have noted, a change in the approach of scholars to Jesus is now taking place along these lines.

I once asked Matthew Black, one of the very best of our New Testament scholars, well known from his book *The Aramaic Origin of the Gospels,* what he thought of a passage in the Jerusalem Talmud where two rabbis are discussing the interpretation of a Hebrew word in Isaiah but did not know how to pronounce it, for they themselves did not speak Hebrew, and so they called in the maid from the kitchen and asked her how she pronounced the word, for she spoke Hebrew. Aramaic was a literary language, but Hebrew, as recent discoveries in archaeology and many newly discovered documents have verified, was the language of the common people. There are certainly Aramaic terms in the Gospels, but when we read that the common people heard Jesus gladly, we must think of him as having spoken to them in the ordinary day-to-day Hebrew with which they were familiar.

The Humanity of Jesus

It has been my custom since I was a child to read through the Bible once or twice a year, and when I come to the Gospels I am always overwhelmed with the thought that here in Jesus it is God himself who has come among us, not just as a man indwelt by the Spirit of God like an Old Testament prophet, but actually *as Man*. I can never get over this astonishing fact. What bowls me over every time I read about Jesus in the Gospels is not the wonderful things he did, not the so-called nature miracles in which the wind and the sea obeyed him, or even his making the dead alive again, for if Jesus really is God, as John Polking-horne the Cambridge mathematical physicist has said, one would expect that, for he was the Creator personally present in the midst of his creation. If you really believe that Jesus is God become incarnate you will have no trouble with the miracles. No! What overwhelms me is the sheer humanness of Jesus, Jesus as the baby at Bethlehem, Jesus sitting tired and thirsty at the well outside Samaria, Jesus exhausted by the crowds, Jesus recuperating his strength through sleep at the back of a ship on the sea of Galilee, Jesus hungry for figs on the way up to Jerusalem, Jesus weeping at the grave of Lazarus, Jesus thirsting for water on the Cross — for that precisely is God with us and one of us, God as "the wailing infant" in Bethlehem, as Hilary wrote, God sharing our weakness and exhaustion, God sharing our hunger, thirst, tears, pain, and death. Far from overwhelming us, God with us and one of us does the very opposite, for in sharing with us all that we are in our littleness and weakness he does not override our humanity but completes, perfects, and establishes it.

What I find always most breathtaking, however, is that in Jesus the Lord God Almighty, the Maker of heaven and earth and of all things visible and invisible, stoops down to be so fully one with us that he speaks to us in our *human* language, and indeed, as Calvin used to say, babbles to us in ways that even children can understand. We don't know what language God speaks in the communion of the Holy Trinity or to the angels and the blessed departed, but we do learn in Jesus that God actually speaks to us in our creaturely language on earth. In Jesus, the Word by whom all things in heaven and earth were created became human and communicates with us and addresses us in this frail crea-turely form.

I will never forget the day after the Russian Sputnik was launched in 1957 when my young sons wanted us to visit Jodrell Bank near

Manchester where the first large radar telescope had been set up by Sir Bernard Lovell. We spent several days there on our way to visit my wife's family in Somerset. We found the radio astronomers in a state of great excitement, not because they were able to track the orbit of the Sputnik round the earth, but because through their radar telescope they were receiving signals from what they regarded at that time to be the outermost edges of the universe. They were so excited that they would not go home to eat or sleep, and their wives had to bring them camp beds and food and drink so that they literally lived in the laboratory for days. With their astonishing radar telescope there was opening out before them the ultimate ranges of the universe revealing its incredible ever-expanding immensity as never before.

Shortly after that we celebrated Christmas at Combe Down in Somerset, and I kept thinking of the fact that the babe born of the Virgin Mary in Bethlehem was none other than God, the Creator and Sustainer of that incredibly vast universe, he for whom the vast galaxies and nebular masses are like dust in the palm of his hand. The Lord God Almighty, Maker of heaven and earth and of all things visible and invisible, had become man in Jesus sharing to the full our littleness and weakness.

How do we link those two facts together? That is the heart of the Christmas message, *Jesus* IS *Immanuel, Jesus* IS *God with us!* Read the first chapter of St. Paul's Epistle to the Colossians; nothing in the whole Bible is more breathtaking than what is written there — the Creator and Upholder of the whole universe of visible and invisible realities is identified with *Jesus,* and in him everything consists and is held together. This truth does not overwhelm or detract from the humanity of Jesus but has the opposite effect. The transcendent deity of Jesus Christ secures and preserves his humanity in a way that no human questioning or critical research can ever undermine.

This, then, is the second thing I wish to stress in preaching Christ as *Jeshua* and *Immanuel: there is an unbroken relation in being and act between Jesus and God.* That was the supreme truth for which Christians had to struggle in the early church, within a culture dominated by the dualist philosophy and science of classical Greece and Rome, which prevented people from thinking of God as interacting with the world or of incarnating himself within it. And it is the same supreme truth for which the Western world has had to fight again and again in face of the dichotomous ways of thinking embedded in our Western philosophy and science, which were given powerful scientific formalization through Newtonian mechanics, for the determinist conception of the universe to which it gave rise led to the deistic notion of a God who does not interact with us in the world of space and time in any realist way.

The Nicene Creed

The ancient world worked with a radical dualism between the sensible world and the intelligible world, or between appearance and reality. When you work with a radical dualism in that kind of way, how can you think of there being an unbroken relationship between Jesus Christ and God? That was not possible within the framework of Greek thought, for it had the effect of driving a sharp line of demarcation between the deity and the humanity of Christ. The whole trend of Greek thinking gave rise to ways of thinking about Jesus which tore him apart and gave rise to the various heresies, all of which in one way or another sinned against the unity of Christ in his person and work, some stressing his deity at the expense of his humanity, and some stressing his humanity at the expense of his deity. That was a way of thinking with which the church had to struggle hard in order to preserve the gospel. And so at the Council of Nicaea the fathers and theologians came up with a theological concept in which they tried to give concise expression to the supreme evangelical truth embedded in the Scriptures of the New Testament, the deity of Jesus Christ who was born of the Virgin Mary and crucified under Pontius Pilate. They knew that if Jesus Christ was not God incarnate, if the relation between Christ and God was severed, the Christian gospel would be emptied of any divine content and would quickly degenerate into some kind of moralistic philosophy with no saving value. And so the church fathers set about finding a way to give decisive expression to the oneness in being and act between Jesus Christ and God the Father. This they did by speaking of Christ as of one and the same being with God the Father. The word for that in Greek was *homoousios* with the Father, the Latin of which is translated as "of the same substance" or as "consubstantial" with the Father. By giving conceptual expression to oneness between the Son of God become man in our world of space and time and God the Creator of heaven and earth and of all visible and invisible reality, the early church set aside at a stroke the epistemological dualism of Greek thought, and did something that penetrated into and changed the very foundations of knowledge in the ancient world. They thereby laid the theological basis for their understanding of the unbroken relation between the sheer humanity of Jesus and God. The history of thought has shown us that it is only when Jesus is known and worshipped as God become man that his humanity has been preserved; when Jesus is detached from oneness with God, what is called "Jesus" is no more than an empty symbol into which people project their own religious fantasies and ideas. That is why the so-called historical Jesus, considered and studied apart from his divine truth, apart from the theological Christ, slips away, as I have said, like sand through people's fingers.

This modernist way of thinking of Jesus is the very opposite of what took place in the ancient times when the church refused to allow Jesus of Nazareth and his intrinsic truth as the incarnate Son of God to be split apart, but took care to hold the historical and the theological factors in the gospel account of Jesus inseparably together. What the ancient church did, then, was in its own way just what Einstein and others have now done in the twentieth century. In their development of general relativity theory and relativistic quantum theory, they have knitted firmly into each other again the empirical and theoretical factors in knowledge which had been split apart in Newtonian physics and mechanics. It was precisely in that way that they laid the foundation for the dynamic understanding of the created universe on which present-day science rests and has made such incredible progress in uniting the subatomic world with the world of the vast immensities of the universe, in uniting microphysics with astrophysics. Behind and below all that lies the great revolution in the foundations of human knowledge in which experience and geometry, physical events and mathematics, or empirical and theoretical factors have been knit together again. That is precisely what the Judeo-Christian theology in the early centuries, in its own sphere and on its own ground, had done long ago, when through bringing together the doctrines of incarnation and creation it overthrew the dualist patterns of thought in Greek philosophy and science and unified understanding in the foundations of knowledge. It was only in that way that they could give faithful theological expression to the key truth upon which the whole gospel of salvation rests, the unbroken relation in being and act between Jesus Christ and God the Father. How interesting and exciting it is that now at last modern science should carry out in its own realm of natural knowledge basically the same revolution in thought that was brought about in theological knowledge in the early centuries of the Christian era under the impact of God's self-revelation in Jesus Christ!

Let us consider the significance of that for a moment. Suppose, for instance, that we think of Jesus as only a man, then what are we to make of his statement to the paralyzed man reported in the second chapter of St. Mark's Gospel, "Your sins are forgiven you," at which the scribes grumbled, for only God can forgive sins? Are the words of Jesus, here and elsewhere, only the words of a man or are they also the words of God? We believe that when Christ says "your sins are forgiven," they really are forgiven. The Jews were right, only God can forgive sins. The whole of the gospel depends on the deity of Christ, for unless he is God, all that Jesus said and did is only of passing ephemeral significance, without any ultimate divine validity. Apart from the deity of Christ, forgiveness or atonement would be null and void.

The One Mediator Between God and Man

The church had to fight hard against the whole thrust of Greek thought to secure this truth that Jesus Christ is God and man and, as such, the

one Mediator between God and man. He really is *Jeshua/Immanuel,*
God with us — when Jesus speaks and acts, God himself is present
speaking and acting. As we have noted, that is the supreme truth that
was secured for the church at the Council of Nicaea in the doctrine of
the *homoousion,* or *consubstantiality,* namely, that *Jesus Christ is of one
being with God the Father.*

However, throughout the centuries the church has had to fight
hard for that very truth again and again. The insidious dualism of pagan
thought crept back into the Western church through the dualistic
thinking of people like St. Augustine in his radical distinction between
the sensible and intelligible realms that came to govern the Latin
concentration on the salvation of the soul and its deliverance from the
world. St. Thomas Aquinas tried to tame that dualism, through Aris-
totelian metaphysics, but all he managed to do was to narrow the gap
between the two realms. Instead of being abolished, however, the dualist
way of thinking of the relation of God to the world became hardened,
so that it was widely held that the Holy Scriptures have to be interpreted
in various figurative ways, for the words of Holy Scripture are not as
such the Word of God. In fact, it was argued, there is no "Word" as
such in God, for when God and the angels or God and the blessed
departed communicate with one another, they do so through the medium of light by way of vision not of word. This had the effect of
undermining the significance of the Holy Scriptures and of throwing
the center of authority upon the institutional church in its interpretation of the Scriptures and upon the word of the church in giving
absolution for sins.

Toward the end of the Middle Ages, however, this view of the
Word was challenged by John Reuchlin, who through his study of
Hebrew gained a very different understanding of what the Word of
God which we hear in the Holy Scriptures really is. He published a
little book called *De Verbo Mirifico (On the Wonderful Word),* in which
he expounded the Hebraic concept of the Word and its identification
with Christ in the New Testament. Then with reference to the teaching
of the Council of Nicaea he argued that since Jesus Christ is the Word
of God as well as the Son of God, we must think of the Word of Jesus

which we hear in the gospel as the incarnate Word of God that is consubstantial with God or of the same substance as God. To deny that there is Word in God is equivalent to rejecting the consubstantiality of Christ the incarnate Son of God. And so John Reuchlin charged mediaeval theology with sinning against the teaching of the Council of Nicaea. This application of the Nicene *homoousion* to the understanding of the Word of God incarnate in Jesus had a profound effect upon people's understanding of the Holy Scriptures as the inspired medium through which we hear the very Word of God, and played a very significant role in the Reformation understanding of the objectivity of the Word of God and of the authority of the Holy Scriptures.

John Major or Mair, a Scot who was then one of the leading theologians in Paris, was asked by the church authorities to examine John Reuchlin's book to see whether it was heretical or not. Major believed Reuchlin to be basically right, and reported that what he taught was in accordance with Nicene Catholic belief. It was current Thomist teaching about the Word that tended to be heretical. If according to the Nicene Creed Jesus Christ is the Son of God, that must also apply to the Word of God made flesh in Jesus Christ. Here, then, at the end of the Middle Ages there was an understanding of the Word of God which radically affected the doctrine of Holy Scripture, even before the Reformation began to revolutionize the understanding of the Bible on the ground that it is the real living Word of God that we hear in the Scriptures, for in them God speaks to us directly and personally.

That encounter with the thought of John Reuchlin left an impact on John Major and influenced his epistemology, but it also influenced the preaching and teaching particularly of the Calvinist Reformation, because, if in the Bible people have to do with a Word that is consubstantial with God, then they read and interpret the Holy Scriptures in quite a different kind of way as the Word of God addressing them directly in and through them.

The Divine Gift and the Divine Giver

A similar change took place during the Reformation in the understanding of the doctrine of grace in the light of the Nicene Creed. In the third article of the Creed belief is confessed in the Holy Spirit, "the Lord and Giver of life who proceeds from the Father and who with the Father and the Son together is glorified and worshipped." In line with what is said there about Jesus Christ as the incarnate Son of God, the Holy Spirit is said to be the Lord and the Giver of Life. In both cases the divine Giver and the divine Gift are one and the same. At the Reformation that Nicene principle was applied not only to the Word of God and to the Spirit of God but also to the grace of God. The grace of God given to us in Christ is not some kind of gift that can be detached from Christ, for in his grace it is Christ himself who is given to us. Properly understood grace is Christ, so that to be saved by grace alone is to be saved by Christ alone. It was in a cognate way that the Reformation (I think here especially of John Calvin) regarded the gift of the Holy Spirit, who is not some gift that can be detached from God and dispensed to us by the church, for the Holy Spirit himself is the Lord and Giver of life. It is through the power of the Holy Spirit that the gift of God in Jesus Christ is mediated to us and we are savingly united to Christ.

Unfortunately, due partly to a confusion between *charis,* the Greek word for grace, and *caritas,* the Latin word for love, there grew up in the Middle Ages the masterful idea that grace is a gift imparted to the church and that the church is endowed with power to dispense that gift. This is a notion of grace as something detached from God, but if the Nicene principle that the gift and the Giver are one applies to grace, as well as to Christ and the Spirit, then it is impossible to think of grace or of the Spirit as endowments bequeathed by Christ to the church to be administered under the authority of the church. Hence, as in the Greek Orthodox Church much earlier, the question was raised by the Reformers whether the church is subjected to God's grace or whether divine grace is subjected to the activity of the church through its clergy. It was the application of the Nicene doctrine of consubstantiality, or the identity between the gift and the Giver, to the doctrine of grace which led the Reformation to depart from that damaging mediaeval conception of grace, and thereby also from the mediaeval notion of the sacraments as "causing grace physically," as Hugo of St. Victor declared.

Three times in its long history the church has had to struggle particularly hard for the supreme truth of the deity of Christ and of the Holy Spirit. *First,* in the fourth century at the Council of Nicaea, when it was realized that if this supreme truth were given up Christianity would lapse back into paganism, or mere secularism and moralism. *Second,* in the sixteenth century in the struggle for the identity between the gift and the Giver, the consubstantiality of grace and of the Word, for it was realized that in that identity the very substance of the gospel was at stake. *Third,* in our own day in the massive upsurge of relativism, secularism, and syncretism, with its lapse back into a deistic disjunction between God and the world and questioning of the uniqueness of Christ, when once again it is the very essence of the Christian faith that is under threat.

The Church's Continuing Struggle Today

We are still in the midst of this struggle to maintain the supreme truth of the unbroken relation in being and act between Jesus Christ and God the Father against insidious dualist or dichotomous ways of thinking, in spite of the fact that in the great scientific revolution of our times those dualist ways of thinking have been comprehensively overcome, at least among the pure sciences. The difficulties facing the preaching of Christ today come, for the most part, from the social sciences, for they still operate with dualist structures of thought and a scientific method that is a hangover from pre-relativity science. This is very evident, for example, in the way they use statistics, which in the final analysis yield determinist patterns of thought and behavior, which has the effect of excluding any thought of God's interaction with the world.

21

Several years ago, when Lord Porter was president of the British Association for the Advancement of Science, he delivered a blistering attack on the social sciences, declaring that they really were not scientific but operated with what he called pseudo-scientific methods. When James Clerk Maxwell began the revolution in scientific explanation and altered the rational structure of science, setting aside the use of mechanical models in research and explanation, he was accused by Lord Kelvin of lapsing into "mysticism"! Maxwell had been brought up to believe in Jesus Christ as the incarnate Son of God through whom the universe had been created and endowed with its contingent rational order and beauty. Already as a teenager being taught Newtonian physics at Edinburgh Academy he began to have difficulties with mechanistic explanations of the way nature behaved. The world of nature that came from the God he knew in Jesus Christ would not have been constructed and/or made to function in that mechanical way. And so even at school he began to work out new ways of scientific thinking, and produced two papers which were deemed to be so good that they were read to the Royal Society of Edinburgh. Later on when, out of deference to Newtonian science, he tried again and again to understand and explain the behavior of light and electromagnetism with the help of mechanical models, he found it impossible, and he developed instead the concept of the continuous dynamic field described in terms of partial differential equations for which he became so famous. He succeeded so well that he laid the foundation for Einstein's theories of special and general relativity. The great Lord Kelvin had taken Maxwell under his wing, but when Maxwell found he had to reject mechanical models, Lord Kelvin accused him of tumbling into "mysticism"! Even in 1905 after Einstein published his epoch-making papers dealing with the behavior of light, Lord Kelvin still insisted, incredibly, that Maxwell's dynamical theory of the electromagnetic field was untenable.

I have taken time to speak about this, because it shows how terribly difficult it is even for a great scientific mind like that of Kelvin to break out of its dogmatism. The mechanistic way of thinking had gained a powerful hold upon the modern mind, and even though that way of thinking has been radically undermined there are still scientists who find it difficult to break out of it — look at the school textbooks on physics! Where it continues to have its biggest hold, however, is in the new social sciences of the twentieth century, which sought to establish themselves as sciences through applying to themselves the old scientific method and the mechanistic ways of thinking that are now so discredited by the pure sciences. No wonder scientists like Lord Porter or Sir Alan Cook have questioned the scientific character, methods, and validity of the social sciences (excluding geography and economics).

Where does the church today stand in all this change? The astonishing thing is that it has almost everywhere allied itself with the social sciences, and with them has laid itself open to the relativism, secularism, and syncretism to which I have already alluded in the struggle of the church to preach Christ and the supreme truth of the gospel. This is all too evident in some of our theological faculties and colleges in the departments of religious studies, where Christian dogmatics is pushed to the wall if it is taught at all. That represents a serious lapse back from rigorous theological science into the kind of rationalistic thinking that arose with the European Enlightenment and prevailed in the nineteenth century, according to which Christianity may be studied and taught in universities only as one religion in a universal class of religions. This implied that the uniqueness of the Christian faith that centers on the person and work of Jesus Christ as the incarnate Son of God could have no place in an academic discipline. Such a rejection of the concrete particularity of the incarnation, of course, was in accord with scientific concern to discover and formulate universal timeless laws of nature through a generalization from particulars. That kind of science had no room for concrete particularities, and it abhorred the very word "singularity." Hence if Christianity was to have an academic place in our universities, the uniqueness of Christ or the concrete particularity of the cross had to be soft-pedalled, to say the least.

The Singularity of the Incarnation

Into the midst of that kind of science a powerful bomb has now been exploded, the discovery of the so-called black hole, the original incredibly dense state of matter from which the universe is held to have expanded with the big bang. With the black hole, however, the concept of *singularity* has bounced back in a very big way and has been radically transforming scientific thinking. My only concern with that here is that *singularity* is now no longer an idea abhorrent to science, but on the contrary a proper scientific concept of absolutely central importance. And as such it has become the great rock of offence upon which the old Enlightenment idea of science concerned with the generating of universal timeless laws has shattered itself, for the universal and the concretely particular have come together with comprehensive significance. The upshot of this is that today scientists are open to the absolute singularity of the incarnation, which they had hitherto rejected out of hand simply because it was a singularity. Many a scientist is now ready for the first time to entertain the Christian concept of the incarnation and to think seriously about the absolute significance of Jesus Christ. And increasingly not a few are ready to believe in him as the way, the truth, and the life apart from whom there is no way to God the Father.

When I published my little book *Space, Time and Incarnation* in 1969 a very distinguished scientist wrote me a letter to thank me for presenting the incarnation and its relation to space and time in a way that he could appreciate and in which he could believe. More than one distinguished scientist has recently become a Christian, for the advance of scientific knowledge has undermined their atheism or their agnosticism — I am constantly hearing of them and sometimes from them. They clamor for a proper understanding of creation and its openness to God. The whole intellectual climate has changed, and scientists are asking theologians to help them think out the interrelation of the incarnation to the creation. They have in mind not least the discovery known as "the anthropic principle," that the expansion of the universe has taken place governed by a very fine tuning of both its strong and its weak forces, which against all the laws of probability has adapted it as the home of humankind. But they also have in mind the fact that, as far as they are able to see, the whole of the universe in its quite incredible immensity is needed for human existence on Planet Earth. Let me refer only to a quite wonderful publication of only thirty-five pages by Professor David Block, the Johannesburg astronomer, called *Our Universe: Accident or Design?*

Unfortunately, however, our theologians and biblical scholars, for the most part at least, are blissfully ignorant of what has taken place and do not seem to believe in the singularity of Christ and the incarnation, and they are therefore unable to help scientists just when they are calling out for it. It seems to be the same case with many of our missionaries who have evidently lost belief in the uniqueness of Christ and speak of Christianity only in the terms of what they call a multifaith approach, in which Christianity is presented along with other religions, as one religion in a universal class of religions, just like the obsolete rationalists of the eighteenth century. One missionary of note who has been trumpeting the singularity of Christ is Lesslie Newbigin. He not only points to the transcendence of Christ but argues that the twin dogmas of the incarnation and the Trinity form the starting point for a way of understanding reality as a whole. It will be sufficient for me here to direct attention to two little books that have come from his pen which all who are concerned with preaching Christ today ought to read: *The Other Side of 1984: Questions for the Churches* and *Foolishness to the Greeks: The Gospel and Western Culture.* What Lesslie Newbigin and his friends are now concerned with is what they call the "gospel as public truth," that is, the evangelization of our modern culture.

Evidence of Change

It may be noted here in passing that events of considerable Christian significance have been taking place in which we see evidence of the winds of God blowing across the churches today. I think particularly of the fact that the doctrine of the Holy Trinity is now becoming the focus of attention again all over the world. I may mention that in 1989 the British Council of Churches published a report of their study commission on trinitarian doctrine today, entitled *The Forgotten Trinity*. And in 1991, after years of discussion beginning in 1976, Orthodox and Reformed churches have produced together an agreed statement on the Holy Trinity. Nothing like this has ever taken place between the churches of the East and West, at least since the early centuries. There is now a rapidly growing literature on the doctrine of the Trinity, with which it is difficult to keep up. I think not least of books discussing ways of bringing Christian understanding of the personal relations within the Holy Trinity to bear upon social relations and structures with a view to bringing about their radical transformation and liberation from fascist and Marxist suppression.

I would like to draw attention to this movement of thought, for there are ways of thinking being pursued today which are not tied up with the Enlightenment rationalism, with the pseudo-sciences, or with relativism and secularism. In connection with the doctrine of the Trinity there become disclosed ways of relational thinking in which even some scientists are becoming very interested, for they find in the Christian doctrine of the Trinity that theologians, as they express it, have been able to map the three to the one and the one to the three, which they need to do but have not been able to do in quantum theory. Moreover, it is when we consider what these scientists call "the intersection of symmetries," between the transcendent order of the divine Trinity and the contingent order of the created universe, that refined patterns of order become disclosed which may very well help scientists when they push their inquiries to the very edge of being, where being bounds on non-being, only to find chaotic states of affairs, which are probably due to the inadequacy of their conceptual instruments (e.g., a mathematics that does not have time relations built into it) as much as to the subtle dynamic nature of reality. If this kind of interrelation between basic theological concepts and basic scientific concepts could be worked out, there might well come about the most profound and startling transformation in human knowledge to the benefit of theological science and natural science alike. This kind of engagement of Christian theology with natural science is, I believe, an essential part of the missionary task of the church in preaching Christ, for evangelization involves not only the evangelization of people but also the evangelization of the structures in which they live and think.

Now let me turn back again to *the unbroken relation in being and act between Jesus Christ and God the Father* upon which the very substance of the gospel rests. Cut the bond of being and act between Jesus Christ and God and the bottom falls out of the gospel, for then all that Jesus was, said, and did is only of transient moral significance. But if Jesus Christ really is God incarnate, and divine and human nature are inseparably united in his one person in an utterly unique way, then Jesus Christ himself in the undiminished fullness of his humanity and deity becomes the very center of the church's mission. To preach Christ to men, women, and children today we must proclaim him in his uncompromising singularity and transcendence as the one Lord and Savior of the world.

So far I have been concerned mainly with the unbroken relation in *being* between Jesus Christ and God. Now let me turn to the oneness in *act* as well as being between Jesus and God.

III

The third thing I would like to speak about in preaching Christ is the cross of Christ. This is the most astonishing part of the Christian message, "God crucified," as Gregory Nazianzen expressed it. The identification of the man on the cross with God himself is, as St. Paul once wrote, offence to the Jews and foolishness to the Greeks. Be that as it may, it is the preaching of Christ crucified that lies at the very center of the Christian gospel if only because the cross, as H. R. Mackintosh once wrote in a gospel tract, is "a window into the heart of God." He was drawing attention there to the words of St. Paul in Romans 8:32: "He who spared not his own Son, but delivered him up for us all, how shall he not with him also freely give us all things." St. Paul was thinking in the back of his mind of the readiness of Abraham to sacrifice his "only son Isaac, whom he loved" (Gen. 22:2, 16), thereby demonstrating that he loved God more than he loved himself. In giving his own dear Son to die for us in atoning sacrifice for the sins of the world, **God has revealed that he loves us more than he loves himself.** Far from remaining detached from us in our fearful alienation and unappeasable agony, God has penetrated through the cross into the deepest depths of our wickedness and violence and taken them all upon himself in order to judge them and redeem us from their tyranny over us.

Let me preface discussion of the cross by referring to my visit to Israel in 1977, where I was warmly welcomed by the President, a distinguished scientist, Professor Katsir, and three ministers from the department of religion who took me to see the *Yad Vashem,* the museum of the Holocaust. I will never forget what I saw and read there. I had been in Palestine, as it was then called, in 1936 when the Grand Mufti came back to Jerusalem from visiting Hitler and spread the terrible poison of his anti-Semitism all over the Middle East. The *Yad Vashem* houses the most detailed account of the abominable murder of millions of Jews through the presentation of written documents, photographs, drawings, including the terrible cartoons of Julius Streicher. I was altogether over-whelmed by the massive evidence vividly placarded before my eyes of the slaughter of six million Jews, which we now know to be an underestimate. When I came out I felt numb with horror and shame that human beings in Christian Europe should have perpetrated such wickedness, and stood still for a few minutes with my three Israeli companions to get my composure. They asked me what I thought about it, and I pointed to a rough-hewn rock outside the entrance, on which there had been fastened some Hebrew words taken from Ezekiel 16 which are cited at every circumcision, "In your blood live." By putting that there, I suggested, you are connecting the blood of Jews slaughtered in the Holocaust with the covenant cut into the flesh of Israel throughout the generations. I added, somehow you have to link God with the Holocaust — if you do not do that, you cannot go on believing in God. All they did was to nod their heads in agreement. Then I said, now I must speak to you as a Christian. That is what we believe to be the significance of the cross of Christ — in him we believe that God himself has come into the midst of our human agony and our abominable wickedness and violence in order to take all our guilt and its just judgment on himself. That is for us the meaning of the cross. If I did not believe in the cross, I could not believe in God. The cross means that, while there is no explanation of evil, God himself has come into the midst of it in order to take it upon himself, to triumph over it and deliver us from it. My three friends were silent, and once more nodded their heads.

Two days later the Mayor of Jerusalem asked one of the leading archaeologists to take my wife and myself round Jerusalem and show what had been carried out. He had been engaged for some years in uncovering historic Jerusalem and opening it up for people to see as never before. The tour on which he took us ended up at the Holy Sepulchre, the place where Jesus was crucified — he had planned it that way. My wife and I knelt down with the pilgrims and prayed, while he stood back. When we got up he took hold of me by the sleeve to pull me aside and said, "I cannot understand why Christians are divided at this place." He understood the reconciling import of the cross of Christ — he, the Jew! But the representatives of different Christian communities at the Holy Sepulchre quarrel with one another so much that the key to the Church of the Holy Sepulchre has to be kept by a Muslim. I learned much from that experience, and I believe more than ever that it is still by the cross of Christ that we Christians can have interrelations with the Jews. But how far is the cross really the controlling center of our own life and thought?

The Power of the Cross

Let me now focus attention on some verses from St. Paul's First Epistle to the Corinthians.

1 Cor. 1:17-18: "For Christ did not send me to baptize but to preach the gospel, and not with eloquent wisdom, lest the cross of Christ

29

be emptied of its power. For the word of the cross is folly to those who are perishing, but to us who are being saved it is the power of God."

1 Cor. 2:2-5: "I decided to know nothing among you except Jesus Christ and him crucified, and I was with you in weakness and trembling, and my speech and my message were not in plausible words of human wisdom but in demonstration of the Spirit and power, that your faith should not rest in the wisdom of men."

It is the cross of Christ that surely lies at the heart of our faith and of the mission of the gospel. I believe that if the church is to be faithful to its calling it must concentrate, as I have said, on the uniqueness of Christ, but on Christ clothed with his gospel as the crucified and risen Lord. It is through the gospel of the saving love of God exhibited and enacted in the atoning sacrifice of Christ that the life and faith of the church are found to be rooted and grounded in the incarnate act of the Son of God in becoming one with us as we really are. He made our lost and damned condition, our death under divine judgment, his very own. I believe we have to stress again the fact that in the incarnation and the cross Christ has penetrated into the darkest depths of our abject human misery and perdition, where he takes our place, intercedes for us, substitutes himself for us, and makes the atoning restitution which we could not make, thereby reconciling us to God in the Holy Spirit as his dear children.

Now in preaching this, I believe that it is concentration upon the *vicarious humanity* of Christ in the incarnation and atonement, in death and resurrection, that is particularly important for us today. It is curious that evangelicals often link the substitutionary act of Christ only with his death, and not with his incarnate person and life — that is dynamite for them! They thereby undermine the radical nature of substitution, what the New Testament calls *katallage*, Christ in our place and Christ for us in every respect. Substitution understood in this radical way means that Christ takes our place in all our human life and activity before God, even in our believing, praying, and worshipping of God, for he has yoked himself to us in such a profound way that he stands in for us and upholds us at every point in our human relations before God.

Galatians 2:20 has long been for me a passage of primary importance as it was for John McLeod Campbell and Hugh Ross Mackintosh: *"I am crucified with Christ, nevertheless I live, yet not I. But Christ lives in me, and the life which I now live in the flesh, I live by the faith of the Son of God, who loved me and gave himself for me."* "The faith of the Son of God" is to be understood here not just as my faith in him, but as the faith of Christ himself, for it refers primarily to Christ's unswerving faithfulness, his vicarious and substitutionary faith which embraces and undergirds us, such that when we believe we must say with St. Paul "not I but Christ," even in our act of faith. This is not in any way to denigrate the human act of faith on our part, for it is only in and through the vicarious faith of Christ that we can truly and properly believe. Faith in Christ involves a polar relation between the faith of Christ and our faith, in which our faith is laid hold of, enveloped, and upheld by his unswerving faithfulness. No human being can do that for another, far less give himself as a ransom from his sin, but this is precisely what the Lord Jesus does when in giving himself for us he completely takes our place, makes our cause his very own in every respect, and yields to the heavenly Father the response of faith and love which we are altogether incapable of yielding.

It is the same conception of faith, I believe, that is found in St. Paul's teaching that we are *justified by faith* and that *the just shall live by faith.* Does this mean that the just person lives from his own faith or from God's faith? In saying that "the just shall live by faith" (Rom. 1:17) the apostle was actually citing from the book of Habakkuk (2:4), but in the Habakkuk Commentary found among the Dead Sea Scrolls this is interpreted to mean that the just live from "the faith of God," which is also, incidentally, the way that people like Athanasius, Calvin, and Barth have interpreted it. However, if we understand faith in the polar way to which I have pointed, justice can be done to both conceptions of faith! In the polar relation the primary pole is certainly God's faith or Christ's faith, for he is the faithful one who lays hold of

31

us and brings us into a living relation with himself, but within the embrace of that relation the secondary pole is that of the believer, his responding faith. But that is an act of faith that is evoked by and sustained by the faithfulness of God — far from being of ourselves, it is a gift of God. This is how, I am sure, we are to understand the relation of our response in faith to the vicarious faith of Christ. The Pauline principle "not I but Christ" applies to faith: "I believe, yet not I but Christ."

The Reconciling Exchange

When preaching about faith in Christ and his vicarious humanity, I sometimes use and develop an illustration taken from John Welsh, the son-in-law of John Knox, who used to point out that our grasping of Christ by faith is itself enclosed within the mighty grasp of Christ, and it is in Christ's grasp of us rather than in our grasp of him that our salvation and certainty lie. In this connection I sometimes recall what happened when my daughter was learning to walk. I took her by the hand to help her, and I can still feel her little fingers tightly clutching my hand. She was not relying on her feeble grasp of my hand, but on my strong grasp of her hand, and even my grasping of her grasping of my hand.

Is that not how we are to understand the faith by which we lay hold of Christ as our Savior? It is thus that our grasp of faith, feeble though it is, is grasped and enfolded in the mighty grasp of Christ, who identifies himself with us and substitutes himself in our place, making what is ours wholly his own, so that we may have wholly made over to us what is Christ's. Think of that in terms of St. Paul's wonderful statement to the Corinthians: "You know the grace of our Lord Jesus Christ, that though he was rich, yet for your sakes became poor, that you through his poverty might be rich" (2 Cor. 8:9). That is what the early church and John Calvin called "the blessed exchange" or "the wondrous exchange," and even the Roman Missal calls *mirabile commercium*. This is in fact the New Testament doctrine of *katallage*, for it is an *atoning and reconciling exchange,* in which what is ours is displaced by Christ who substituted himself in our place and yet is restored in a new way to us.

A very important point must be noted here, relating to the fact that in his becoming one of us and one with us as we actually are, *Christ takes our sins upon himself in such a way as to make them serve our healing and salvation.* Think of the incident in the Gospel when James and John quite selfishly asked for the privilege of being at the right hand and left hand of Jesus at the inauguration of his kingdom, which made the other disciples angry. Jesus did not rebuke them, except to ask if they could drink of the cup that he drank of and be baptized with the baptism with which he was baptized. When they said they could, he promised that they would indeed drink of the cup that he drank of and be baptized with the baptism with which he was baptized (Mark 10:35-40).

A little later, Jesus sat down with his disciples at the Passover meal at which he specifically *linked his body and blood with the covenant.* Then when Jesus was betrayed and crucified the disciples found themselves in utter disarray, standing before the cross in a crowd of people who mocked and jeered at Jesus and laughed at the helplessness of Jesus nailed to the cross. Jesus was now utterly alone, abandoned by them, and the disciples were now separated from him by an unbridgeable chasm of shame and betrayal and horror, for they had all forsaken him and fled. They had betrayed the very love with which he had bound them to himself. Then they remembered what had happened in the upper room and the covenant Jesus had forged with them in his body and blood. **Jesus had meant them to remember, for in that act he took their very sins, even their denial of him, and used it as the very means by which to bind them to himself.**

Then the disciples understood the significance of the vicarious Passion of Christ as something undertaken not for the righteous, but precisely for the sinner. It was their very sin, their betrayal, their shame, their unworthiness, which became in the inexplicable love of God the very material he laid hold of and turned into the bond that bound them to the crucified Messiah, to the salvation and love of

God forever. *That is the way in which the* katallage, *the wondrous exchange of the atoning and reconciling cross of Christ, operates, by making the shameful things that divide us from him into the very things that bind us to him in life and death forever. Such is the unlimited power of the cross of Christ.*

The Gospel at the Lord's Supper

It is not easy to preach the truth that we are saved by the grace of Christ alone and that it is through the vicarious humanity of Jesus and in its substitutionary bearing upon faith that we can properly believe, but this is what may be proclaimed at Holy Communion as nowhere else. In our Scottish tradition the great revivals have often taken place in connection with the celebration of the Lord's Supper, for example, the great revival in the middle of the eighteenth century at Shotts Kirk (where, incidentally, my grandparents are buried).

I have found in my own ministry that it is easiest to preach the unconditional nature of grace, and the vicarious humanity and substitutionary role of Christ in faith, at the celebration of the Eucharist, where the call for repentance and faith is followed by Communion in the body and blood of Christ in which we stretch out empty hands to receive the bread and wine: "Nothing in my hands I bring, simply to thy Cross I cling." There at the holy table or the altar I know that I cannot rely on my own faith but only on the vicarious faith of the Lord Jesus in the total substitution of his atoning sacrifice on the cross. Salvation and justification are by the grace of God alone. Faith, as John Calvin taught, is an empty vessel, so that when you approach the table of the Lord, it is not upon your faith that you rely, but upon Christ and his cross alone. That is what the covenant in his body and blood which the Savior has forged for us actually, practically, and really means. It is of the very essence of the gospel that salvation and justification are by the grace of Christ alone, in which he takes your place, that you may have his place.

I believe this emphasis in the mission of the church may well be more important than anything else in Scotland today. There is a kind of subtle Pelagianism in preaching and teaching which has the effect of throwing people back in the last resort on their own act of faith, so that in the last analysis responsibility for their salvation rests upon themselves, rather than on Christ. In far too much preaching of Christ the ultimate responsibility is taken off the shoulders of the Lamb of God and put upon the shoulders of the poor sinner, and he knows well in his heart that he cannot cope with it. Is that not one of the things that keeps pushing people away from the church? I think here of the reluctance of many people in the Highlands to approach the holy table, but this is something that sadly happens all over the land when people fail to understand the absolutely free and unconditional nature of the grace of the Lord Jesus Christ, who came to call not the righteous but sinners to repentance, and who through the miracle of his cross turns our sins and failings into the very means he uses in order to save us and bind us to himself — that is precisely what he pledges to us in the Communion of his body and blood.

Unconditional Grace

Let us pause for a minute to reflect on the nature and implications of unconditional grace as it is freely extended to us in forgiveness. One does not forgive an innocent person but only a guilty one — by its very nature forgiveness involves a judgment on the wrongdoer. Total forgiveness involves total judgment, and it is total forgiveness that Christ gives us which involves a total judgment upon us. Think of that in terms of the cross, on which Christ died for us, all of us, and the whole of each one of us, not just a part of us. Hence we must think that the whole of our being comes under the judgment of the cross. That is why, as H. R. Mackintosh used to say, at the Lord's Supper as we partake of the body and blood of Christ, we feel ashamed of our whole being, our goodness as well as our badness. In the atoning exchange of grace in which Christ gave himself for us, *all* that we are and claim to be is called in question. There is no such thing as a partial substitution, or

35

therefore a partial forgiveness and a partial judgment. Each one of us comes unreservedly under the judgment of the cross, for in his act of total self-substitution Christ took the place of each one of us in making our sin his own and in bearing it along with the judgment of God upon it. Christ Jesus died for us when we were yet sinners; hence we must think of him as having died for all people while they are yet sinners irrespective of their response. Just as the cross is proclaimed to all, so the total forgiveness and the total judgment it involves are proclaimed to all, whether they believe or not. But unconditional forgiveness involves unconditional judgment. Just as divine forgiveness is not given on the ground of some condition being met by us, so the judgment it involves, the judgment enacted and exhibited on the cross once for all, is likewise unconditioned.

This unconditional grace of the Lord Jesus Christ which is proclaimed to us in the gospel summons us to repent and believe. But in our very act of believing and repenting, *we* with our faith, with our believing and repenting *self,* come under the unconditional judgment of Christ's forgiveness. Face to face with the Lord Jesus, whose eyes search out the deepest secrets of our being and whose Spirit discerns the thoughts and intents of the heart, all our acts of faith and repentance, our prayer and worship, are found to be unclean in God's sight, so that if divine forgiveness were conditional on our responses, we would never be saved. Even the exercise of our free will in believing and repenting in response to the summons of the gospel is not separable from our self-will, for it is the *self* in our free will and self-will, the subtle Pelagianism of the human heart, that comes under the judgment of Christ's unconditional forgiveness. We sinful human beings are trapped by our sin within the circle of our hearts which are turned in upon themselves, so that we cannot even repent of our faith or repent of our repentance, but are cast wholly and unreservedly upon the unconditional forgiveness of Christ Jesus. Indeed, it is because the judgment inherent in his forgiveness falls upon the innermost self in all our acts of faith and repentance that we are thrown upon Christ alone and are saved by grace alone.

Without any doubt the gospel of unconditional grace is very

difficult for us, for it is so costly. It takes away from under our feet the very ground on which we want to stand, and the free will which we as human beings cherish so dearly becomes exposed as a subtle form of self-will — no one is free to escape from his self-will. It is the costliness of unconditional grace that people resent. Martin Luther once said that when he preached justification by faith alone, people responded to it like a cow staring at a new gate, but he also said that when he preached justification by grace alone it provoked tumults. I find this kind of disturbance again and again in the reaction not only of people outside the church but even of would-be evangelical people within the membership of the church, for their refusal to accept unconditional grace seems to be due to the fact that it cuts so deeply into the quick of their souls. This is part of what I meant a short time ago when I pointed out that there is a subtle form of Pelagianism in the way people often preach the gospel and claim that people will be saved only if they believe, or on condition that they believe. Hidden deep down beneath all that there is a failure to take the New Testament teaching about the power of the cross of Christ and his substitutionary role seriously, a reluctance to allow it to apply to the whole of their being and to all their human activity before God, even to their believing and praying and worshipping. We need to learn and learn again and again that salvation by grace alone is so radical that we have to rely upon Christ Jesus entirely in everything, and that it is only when we rely on him alone that we are really free to believe: "Not I but Christ" yet "Christ in me." Because he came as man to take our place, in and through his humanity our humanity is radically transformed, and we become truly human and really free to believe, love, and serve him. That is the wonderful message of the cross and resurrection.

I have been laying the emphasis upon the unconditional nature of salvation by grace grounded in the fact that Christ gave himself freely in atoning sacrifice for all people without exception, for that is what we are sent by our Lord to preach. But what of those who turn away from the gospel and its summons to repent and believe? They do not thereby nullify the unconditional nature of the grace of Christ, or therefore the unconditional nature of the divine judgment which it involves. The judgment of God upon sinners remains when they spurn his grace. While the preaching of the gospel, in the vivid expression of St. Paul, is to some people a vital fragrance that brings life, to others it is a deadly fume that kills (2 Cor. 2:16). That is to say, if people are damned, they are damned by the gospel. Why anyone who is freely offered the unconditional grace and love of God in the Lord Jesus should turn away from him is something quite inexplicable and baffling to those who are "on the way to salvation," but it is a fearful fact that the New Testament will not allow preachers of the gospel to ignore or forget its teaching about damnation. It is at the final judgment that the dark side of the cross, the unconditional judgment of God upon all sin and evil, will be unveiled, for people will be judged by what took place once for all in the finished work of Christ on the cross, when he was crucified as the Lamb of God to bear and bear away the sins of the world. Is that not what the New Testament speaks of as "the wrath of the Lamb"?

It was one of the lovely and refreshing things about the preaching of Billy Graham in Scotland recently that in preaching Christ he directed people to Christ and to Christ alone as Lord and Savior, in such a direct and blunt way, not through brilliant preaching, that through the Holy Spirit thousands and thousands of people who were not members of the church, and thousands who were under thirty years of age, were challenged by the gospel and turned in their utter help-lessness to Christ Jesus, to find in him one who has wholly taken their place so that they might freely be given his place. It is in this message of the unconditional grace and vicarious humanity of the Lord Jesus Christ that people have often told me that they have found the healing and liberation which they never thought possible.

The Wisdom and Power of God

Let me now end by directing attention back to those two passages in Paul's First Epistle to the Corinthians (1:17-18; 2:2-5) and through them to the cross of Christ as the power of God and to the kind of faith that does not stand in the wisdom of human beings but in the power of God.

I believe that emphatic focus upon this truth is precisely what is very much needed in the church today in its calling to preach Christ. This is the central truth that we must surely stress in the ministry of ministers, and elders, and deacons, and church workers alike, and in the Christian witness of every member of the church. It is the one message that really reaches the multitudes that are outside the church, the young as well as the old. Unfortunately the kind of evangelism that is so often most vociferous actually seems to blur the radical nature of Christ's vicarious humanity and the New Testament gospel that proclaims it. That kind of "evangelism" itself needs to be evangelized! The gospel must be proclaimed in an evangelical way! It is the proclamation of the cross as the power of God, and teaching about faith standing in the power of God and not in the wisdom of human beings, foolish as it may look before the wisdom of the world, that will open wide the gates and point the way ahead for a radical renewal of the church and its mission. That is the kind of wisdom, the wisdom of God, as St. Paul called it, that we in the church desperately need today.

In the celebration of the Eucharist in the Orthodox Church, it is when the holy gospel is lifted up and carried forth that there rings out through the church a loud shout from the priest standing in front of the congregation, "Here is Wisdom." Yes, it is in the celebration of the Eucharist or the Lord's Supper that proclamation of the Lord's death and the wisdom of God come so effectively together in the life and ministry of the church, for it is at the Eucharist, where we rely wholly upon Christ and his cross, not at all upon ourselves, that true wisdom is to be found, the wisdom of God!

*　　*　　*

Increase, O God, the faith and the zeal of all your people, that they may earnestly desire and more diligently seek the salvation of their fellow-men through the message of your love in Jesus Christ our Lord. Send forth a mighty call to your servants to preach your Word, and multiply the number of those who labor in the Gospel; granting to them a heart of love, sincerity of speech, and the power of the Holy Spirit, that they may be able to persuade people to forsake sin and turn to you. And so bless and favor the work of your evangelists, that multitudes may be brought from the kingdom of evil into the Kingdom of your dear Son, our Savior Jesus Christ.

(Prayers for Divine Service)

Incarnation and Atonement in the Light of Modern Scientific Rejection of Dualism

Address to the Theological Students' Forum,
Princeton Theological Seminary, April 9, 1992

L et me explain to you the choice of the subject. I am a member of two international academies, *Académie Internationale des Sciences Religieuses* and *Académie Internationale de Philosophie des Sciences,* based in the Palais des Académies, Brussels. Members of the former are for the most part theologians and biblical scholars. The second academy is not composed of philosophers but mainly of scientists and mathematicians who are also concerned with the epistemology of science. Some of us are members of both academies, which sometimes hold joint sessions. Because members of the two academies rub shoulders with one another we find that we share problems which cut across the concerns of both academies. The big problem that keeps on arising is that philosophers, theologians, and biblical scholars often tend to be trapped within dualist patterns of thought which scientists on the whole have rejected. They have their problems, too, in the tension that arises between their critical realism and the epistemological presuppositions latent in the Copenhagen-Göttingen forms of quantum theory. I think here, for example, of the great John Wheeler of Princeton and of Bernard D'Espagnat and Costa de Beauregard, two quantum physicists of France who tend still in my view to be somewhat dualist in their adherence to the teaching of Niels Bohr. However, by and large the thinking of scientists has undergone a radical change since the epistemological revolution brought about by general relativity theory. And here I think particularly of the contribution of Ilya Prigogine, another one of our members, who is particularly concerned with non-equilibrium thermodynamics and the role of time as an internal operator in mathematical equations, not as an external geometric parameter, which it is in traditional Newtonian science.

Let me try to say something about this change going on in the foundations of knowledge. In general relativity theory physics and geometry are integrated so that one does not operate with an independent conceptual system prior to one's actual physics — that dualism was comprehensively destroyed by Einstein. As a result scientists think from beginning to end in terms of the integration of empirical and theoretical factors, both in nature and in our knowledge of it. This represents an immense epistemological revolution in which ontology and epistemology are now wedded together. That is a development which biblical scholars by and large have not yet appreciated, for many of them are still stuck in old Enlightenment, pre-Einsteinian ways of thinking. This is to a certain extent due to the massive genius of Immanuel Kant, through whom the dualism built into modern classical science by Galileo and Newton was given a metaphysical form that has had a powerful influence on modern thought.

Now let me refer to one of the problems that arises out of that development, which we discussed in the Academy of the Philosophy of Sciences when two years ago I was asked to read a paper on "Time in Scientific and Historical Research." Wilhelm Herrmann of Marburg, still working within the dualist frame of thought, drew a distinction with which many of us are very familiar between *Historie* and *Geschichte*. *Historie* is the type of history in which historical events are interpreted in terms of the causal connections or external relations between them. If that is given primacy then from the *historisch* point of view you set aside all divine revelation, all God's interaction with us in the world, and so all miracles as violations of natural law. That of course is the approach that Rudolf Bultmann adopted in his interpretation of the New Testament. Along with this went another concept of history to which Bultmann and many biblical scholars, but not secular historians, subscribed. This is a *geschichtlich* way of understanding historical events, which interprets them in terms of what they mean for us today. This

42

distinction between *Historie* and *Geschichte* ultimately goes back to Newton when he differentiated between *absolute mathematical time and space,* which govern all causal interpretations of phenomena, and *relative apparent time and space,* which have to do with phenomena or appearances. That was the dualism that lay behind Lessing's famous distinction between "necessary truths of reason" and "accidental truths of history," which along with Kant's phenomenalism has influenced Bultmann and many biblical scholars, who to this day have not yet broken free from it. It was built into the historical-scientific method which, as far as I can see, is neither truly scientific nor truly historical. This is a matter which I have discussed a number of times, not least in its bearing upon the nature of *time.* Several years ago, for example, I contributed an essay on this subject to a festschrift for Jürgen Moltmann, in which I called for a radically new and more scientific way of handling history in the light of the role of dynamical field-theory which we owe to James Clerk Maxwell and of space-time which we owe to Albert Einstein.

Our problem today is that, in spite of the great advance made in the exact sciences, contemporary culture is still anachronistically affected by the dualism of the Enlightenment, which is particularly evident in the social sciences, but also in the biblical and theological sciences that often tend to take their cue from them. During the Enlightenment there was posited a very radical split between the "is" and the "ought," and between the "how" and the "why." It is that very split that our scientists, working in the epistemological foundations of their knowledge, now find that they are forced to question when they probe into the ultimate rational ground upon which the laws of nature rest. They have to find ways of overcoming that deep split posited by the Enlightenment, which is not easy to do. For example, the moral imperative has somehow to be built into the basic structure of natural or physical law, for rigorous science by its very nature cannot operate under the constraint of any external authority. That is not easy to do, but papers are now appearing, written mainly by physicists, on this very matter.

Let me refer particularly to the spiritual problem that has arisen for us in theology. When you work with a dualist pattern of thought you not only divide between God and the world, and thereby deny any interaction between God and the world, but in the end you operate with a damaging split between Jesus Christ and God, which is spiritually and pastorally disastrous. The pursuit of so-called natural theology has had a good deal to do with that. When with the Enlightenment there arose as a result of dualist thinking a deistic disjunction in thought between God and the universe, there took place a resurgence of natural theology which has always arisen in the great periods of dualist thought, as in the medieval and the post-Newtonian eras, when people tried to build a logical bridge between God and the world and between faith and reason. A great deal of modern apologetics from both the liberal and the fundamentalist camps is in different ways tied in with that. However, such a logical bridge between God and the world, and indeed between being and statement, has now been comprehensively demolished, not just by the rigorous theology of Karl Barth, but by the profound revolution in logic that has taken place, in which it has been made clear that it is impossible to state in statements how statements relate to being, without resolving everything into statements. Most theologians, however, I am sorry to say, have not begun to appreciate the far-reaching significance of this revolution.

There are of course also some scientists who fail to appreciate the epistemological implications of this revolution by clinging to a phenomenalist conception of scientific method in which attention is first given to the establishing of empirical data, and then to the development of theoretical concepts by way of deduction from empirical data. Most scientists, however, while holding that scientific concepts have reference to sensible experiences, realize that they are simply not deducible from them, for, as Einstein showed, they are *ontologically*, not logically, derived, and as Michael Polanyi and Karl Popper among others have shown there is no logic of scientific discovery. Anyhow, it has become very clear from this point of view that the structures of so-called natural theology which some people still try to build up between God and the world cannot stand up to critical analysis and inevitably collapse — they presuppose a deistic disjunction between God and the world which cannot be bridged over by logical operations.

So much, then, by way of introduction indicating why I have framed the title of this address "Incarnation and Atonement in the Light of Modern Scientific Rejection of Dualism."

I would now like to do three things. First of all I want to talk about the nature of scientific inquiry, because many people are still worried about the interrelation between science and theology. Secondly, I want to ask how the early church coped with the problem of dualism in laying the foundations of Christian theology. And then, in the third place, I want to ask what we are to do today in the light of modern scientific rejection of dualism.

The Nature of Scientific Inquiry

Here I have learned as much from the great fathers of the church, people like Athanasius or Cyril of Alexandria, as I have from modern theologians like Karl Barth or modern scientists like James Clerk Maxwell, Albert Einstein, or Michael Polanyi, or from philosophers like John Macmurray. You can express it basically in this way. In any rigorous scientific inquiry you pursue your research in any field in such a way that you seek to let the nature of the field or the nature of the object, as it progressively becomes disclosed through interrogation, control how you know it, how you think about it, how you formulate your knowledge of it, and how you verify that knowledge. I often speak of this as *kataphysic inquiry,* a term that comes from the Greek expression κατὰ φύσιν, which means "according to nature." If you think of something in accordance with its nature like that, you think of it in accordance with what it *really* is — so that here thinking κατὰ φύσιν is to think κατ᾽ ἀλήθειαν. Hence in this context the terms φύσις and ἀλήθεια, nature and reality, are really equivalent. This way of thinking had already been developed in Alexandrian science by the so-called φυσικοί ("physical" or natural scientists), who insisted on *asking positive questions or framing thought experiments designed to disclose the nature of the realities* into which they inquired, but because they were questions that yielded *positive answers governed by the nature of those realities,* those

45

"physical" or natural scientists were nicknamed "dogmatics" or δογ-
ματικοί by sceptical philosophers like Sextus Empiricus. Thus there
arose especially in Alexandria the conception of "dogmatic science," or
ἐπιστήμη δογματική, to describe rigorous scientific inquiry conducted
strictly in accordance with the nature or reality of things. This applied
to every field of inquiry, and that was how theological inquiry concerned
with the nature and activity of God was viewed by the great theologians
in the ancient church, which they often spoke of as ἐπιστήμη δογματική, or "dogmatic science."

Moreover, when under the impact of Christian theology the nature of the created universe was regarded as *contingent*, even in its
rational order, the foundations were laid, as we now know, upon which
all empirico-theoretical science ultimately rests. Since the universe has
been given a reality of its own which, while contingent upon God, is
utterly different from him, it cannot be known through *a priori* reasoning but may be known only out of itself, as it discloses its own
nature to us in answer to experimental or physical interrogations.

Let me indicate how this rigorous scientific inquiry operates. Suppose we inquire into the nature of a tree and bring all our rational faculties
to bear upon it. In doing so we develop a modality of the reason that is
appropriate to the specific nature of the tree and do not treat the tree as
we would a rock or a human being, for that would be to think of it
contrary to its nature, παρὰ φύσιν, as the Greeks would say. A tree is alive
but not personally alive, and so we adapt our mode of knowing and
reasoning in accordance with its nature as a tree. Suppose then we switch
our inquiry to a cow, which is a living thing like a tree but is an animal,
which unlike a tree is a moving being. Here there takes place another
switch in the modality of our reason, in which it is adapted to the specific
nature of the cow as an animal. Our scientific method is the same,
knowing something as rigorously as possible in accordance with its
nature. But when we then turn our inquiry toward a human being, the
modality of our reason changes yet again in accordance with the nature
of the human being. Here a radical change is involved because unlike a
cow a human being can talk back to us and reveal something of himself
or herself to us. Moreover, a human being is a rational agent with a depth

of intelligibility that a cow does not have, and a human being is personal in nature, which calls for a two-way relation, a personal interaction, between the knower and the one known. We cannot get to know another human being if we stand aloof and say, now just you keep dumb, and let me try and understand you. We cannot really know another human being except in a two-way interaction with him or her. We have to open our heart and mind to him or her and listen to what he or she has to say about himself or herself. It is only in and through personal interaction that we get to know another human being. In fact, we probably really know others only as we reveal ourselves to them, rather than merely by trying to find out what they are in themselves by way of impersonal observation and deduction.

Then let us switch the modality of our reason to God. Now here we have an even more radical change, because God is the Creator and Lord and we are creatures who, while personal, are utterly different from him in the nature of our being. Hence with God we have to do with a kind of relation which is quite different from that which we have with other creatures. With trees or animals we have to do with objective realities over which we can exercise some control in varying degrees as we subject them to our inquiries, but when we turn attention to other human beings we are not in a position to exercise control over them. A human being is personally other than we are and is more profoundly objective than a tree or a cow, for he or she would object to our attempts to control them. Here, then, we have to do with a measure of objectivity that we do not have with other creatures. But when we turn our attention to God we have to do with a relation of the profoundest objectivity which we can never master. He is the Lord God before whom our human knowing undergoes a radical change, which I sometimes speak of as an *epistemological inversion* of our ordinary knowing relation. We can know God only through his self-revelation and grace, and thus only in the mode of worship, prayer, and adoration in which we respond personally, humbly, and obediently to his divine initiative in making himself known to us as our Creator and Lord. Here the modality of our reason undergoes radical adaptation in accordance with the compelling claims of God's transcendent nature — that is precisely what authentic theology involves. This is very important because it calls for a real change in the whole structure of our soul and mind in our approach to God, and as often as not it is a painful change in which the self-centered structure of our minds is turned inside out and transformed. Apart from such a μετάνοια or deep-seated change in mind and heart, you cannot really be a theological student, far less a minister of the gospel. No wonder our Lord Jesus told his followers that they must renounce themselves and take up their cross daily if they were to be his disciples. Does that not in its way also describe the kind of repentant rethinking of all unwarranted presuppositions and the objective commitment to the truth which characterize rigorous scientific inquiry?

If we regard science in this rigorous way, and hold theology also to be a rigorous science (as I do), how are they to be related to one another? Think of it like this. The theologian and the scientist live and work within the same room, so to speak, within the same empirical world of space and time, which both the theologian and the scientist have to take seriously. The theologian is concerned with God as he reveals himself to us within space and time through historical Israel and in the incarnation of his Word in Jesus Christ, so that we cannot divorce what God reveals to humankind from the medium of spatio-temporal structures which he uses in addressing his Word to human beings. Empirical correlates therefore have an ineradicable place in theology, as in natural science — hence theological truths and concepts may not be resolved away or "demythologized" without losing their essential content or import. The scientist on his part is concerned in his inquiries only with events and forces which have space-time coordinates and only with theoretical concepts, however abstruse, that are empirically correlated with space and time. Within the same sphere of space and time which both share, the scientist inquires into the nature of created realities, but the theologian inquires into the nature of God, the Creator of those realities. When the scientist inquires into the nature of the world, he does that not by looking at God but by looking away from him at the world, but when the theologian inquires into the nature of God as he has revealed himself he does that not by looking at the nature of the world, which God has created out of nothing, but by looking away from the world to its Creator. The scientist and the theologian thus move in opposite directions. The scientist is concerned with the created or contingent universe, so that he does not reckon God among the data with which natural science is concerned. And that is of course consonant with a proper theological understanding of the nature of the universe which God has created as a reality utterly different from himself but which he has endowed with a created rational order reflecting his own transcendent rationality. This is part of the Christian doctrine of contingence, upon the truth of which in the last analysis empirical science and its historical development rest.

Let me repeat, since both the scientist and the theologian pursue their inquiries within the same structures of space and time, there is inevitably an overlap in their inquiries. In that case there must be some basic connection between the concepts of natural science, which are spatio-temporal, and the concepts of theological science, which for all their difference have spatio-temporal ingredients. This is particularly evident in the doctrine of the incarnation, in which Christian theology is concerned with the coming of God himself into space and time and becoming one of us in space and time, without of course ceasing to be God. He does not abrogate space and time but on the contrary supports, qualifies, and reinforces space and time, and indeed is concerned with healing what happens within our space-time world and delivering it from disorder. Thus the incarnation and the atonement cannot be expounded except as involving space-time coordinates. Here, however, space and time, in anticipation of modern science, are to be understood in a *relational* way, and Greek container concepts are set aside (e.g., the concept of space in the fourth book of Aristotle's *Physics*). I shall come back to this point later.

Theological Inquiry in the Early Church

Theologians in the early centuries of the Christian era had to cope with very difficult problems not unlike those we have in the modern world. The questions that they faced had to do to a large extent with the radical dualism that affected all classical culture, that is, Greco-Roman culture, in which a sharp line of demarcation or separation, a χωρισμός, was drawn between the intelligible realm and the sensible realm, that is, a realm of eternal ideas and a realm of empirical events, or a realm of reality and a realm of appearance. Consequently for the Greeks anything that took place in the empirical or phenomenal realm was regarded as lacking in reality, as evanescent appearance, and even as evil. The only realm to which scientific attention could be directed was the intelligible realm of eternal and necessary forms that are not affected by the decay and unreality of this passing world. Within an outlook of that kind, governed by a radical disjunction between reality and appearance, the eternal and the temporal, the heavenly and the earthly, the intelligible and the sensible, the teaching of the Bible, particularly of the New Testament about God becoming incarnate and acting in the sensible material world, could only be regarded by the Greeks as a crude mythological way of thinking. Thus the message of the gospel, interpreted within the dualist framework of thought prevailing in the culture of the Mediterranean world, was regarded as a mythological way of thinking in which irrational facts and events from this passing world of appearance are wrongly projected into the real world of eternal forms and timeless truth.

It was Athanasius above all who showed the church that it is the axiomatic assumption of a radical dichotomy between a realm of events and a realm of ideas that gives rise to a mythological way of thinking, but that false assumption was demolished by the fact that in Jesus Christ the eternal Logos of God had become incarnate in our physical existence. This had the double effect of de-divinizing the rational forms of Greek thought and of affirming the reality of the empirical world of space and time, which must therefore be regarded as worthy of rational or scientific attention. Do not be beguiled by the idea that a myth is but a primitive, picturesque way of expressing truth. That is spread around today, but it is only a device by which modern mythological thinking evades the realist thrust of divine revelation and activity in space and time. In ancient times the theologians of the church found that in order to get the message of the gospel across to the world they had to find ways of overthrowing dualistic habits and patterns of thought and replacing them with a unitary understanding of the created universe of heaven and earth and of God's redemptive interaction with it. That is still our task today, but, as we shall see, it is the advance of science in modern times that has been demolishing dualistic ways of thinking and developing realist but open-structured ways of understanding the unitary rational order manifest throughout the universe.

Before we go more deeply into things, let me indicate briefly and diagrammatically the kind of problems that arise here. Picture in your mind the three ways in which two hemispheres may be related to one another: (1) as adjacent to one another but with a clear gap between them; (2) as touching one another tangentially; and (3) as intersecting one another or overlapping with one another. (1) and (2) presuppose a dualist framework of thought, whereas (3) rejects dualism in favor of interactionism.

Consider first (1) and (2). (1) describes a radical disjunction between the divine and earthly realms, which is found in Gnostic literature. That disjunction was so wide that the gap between them had to be bridged by semi-divine beings. This was fiercely combatted by the Christian theologians of the third century, for in its different forms it made nonsense of the gospel — for example, in the sharp antithesis posited by Marcion between a Creator God and a Redeemer God, or in the mythological projection of intermediaries between the earthly and heavenly spheres. (2) on the other hand also describes a disjunction between the divine and the human, the heavenly and earthly, but one in which the two realms are held to relate to one another merely tangentially without in any way intersecting one another. That is to say, they touch one another at a mathematical point, but since such a mathematical point is dimensionless, there can be myriads of them. That is precisely how the Arians conceived of the way in which the realm of God and the realm of this world touch one another tangentially at the point called "Christ." Since that is a dimensionless mathematical point, Arius claimed that there must be "myriads" of such "Christs" or images of God. "Christ" is then ultimately no more than a creaturely, transient, this-worldly symbol of the divine without objective divine

51

content. (3) in contrast to (1) and (2) describes a relation between the two hemispheres or realms in which they intersect with one another, so that there is an area in which the content of one belongs to the content of the other.

How do we within this phenomenal or empirical world know God in Christ if in him we have no more than a tangential relation to the divine? How can we know God through Christ if Christ is not also on the divine side of that boundary between man and God, and if in Christ human inquiry is unable to cross over the boundary and really terminate upon God beyond? If we in this creaturely world try to make sense of Christ when the human and the divine only bear upon one another tangentially, our attempts to think of God inevitably bend back upon ourselves, so that we interpret Christ and God through Christ out of our preconceptions and in terms of our own self-understanding. That is precisely how Athanasius regarded the mythological thinking of the Arians, contrasting it with proper and accurate thinking of God on the ground of his objective self-revelation to us in Jesus Christ, the incarnate Son of God. If you try to think accurately of God, he argued, you have to think κατὰ διάνοιαν, across or away from yourselves toward God, but the mythologizing Arians thought of God κατ' ἐπίνοιαν, out of themselves, for in the end all they can say about God is of their own devising, excogitated out of their own self-understanding. If in our world today (1) may be said to represent or correspond in some measure to the thought of Paul Tillich, (2) may be said to represent or correspond to the thought of Rudolf Bultmann, who, operating with a sharp disjunction between *Jenseits* and *Diesseits,* the other world and this world, interpreted the teaching of the New Testament not in terms of God's objective self-revelation but mythologically in terms of humankind's existential self-understanding.

The teaching of Gnostics and Arians in different ways gave the early church a great deal of trouble, for the dualism that lay behind it threatened to undermine the gospel of God's objective revealing and saving activity in Jesus Christ and reduce it to a merely symbolical and mythological way of thinking, as we have noted. In the conflicts that arose it soon became apparent to the church fathers that if they were to proclaim that in Jesus Christ God had become man for us and our salvation and communicate that within the world of Greek culture, philosophy, and science, and if the Christian message was to be received and understood and to take root in the Mediterranean world, they had to do something that destroyed the dualism and changed the foundations of knowledge. That is indeed what they did do in giving decisive formulation to the incarnation in our physical world of the Word or Logos of God by whom all things visible and invisible have been made. Thereby, let it be said again, they discounted the Greek notion of the unreality of the physical realm and showed at the same time that the rational forms of thought venerated by the Greeks as divine and timeless were the created forms of rationality with which the Creator had endowed the universe.

Christians taught that in Jesus Christ God himself has come into our world and become man, yet without ceasing to be God. He is a creature of our world and yet the Creator by whom all things are made. He is true God of God and yet true man of man, so that when we know God in Jesus Christ our knowledge terminates on the very Being of God, and not just on the being of man. This carried with it two very fundamental principles: that Jesus Christ the incarnate Son of God is of one and the same being (ὁμοούσιος) as the Father, and that in Jesus Christ divine and human natures are united in one person (ἕνωσις ὑποστατική). It was on the basis of that teaching that the great theologians of the fourth century destroyed the epistemological and cosmological dualisms endemic in Hellenic culture and transformed the foundations of knowledge, and incidentally laid the basis upon which our modern empirico-theoretical science rests.

Let me indicate the evangelical significance of what took place, for it had to do with the supreme truth of the Christian faith, the deity of Jesus Christ, which the Council of Nicaea was concerned to defend and substantiate against heretical subversion. If there is no ontological bond between Jesus Christ and God, if he is just a man on earth speaking about God, then what about the message of the gospel when Jesus says, "Son, daughter, your sins are forgiven"? If that is merely the word of a man and not of God then sins are not forgiven, for such a word of "forgiveness" is without any divine validity. Hence to cut the bond between Jesus and God is to tear the very heart out of the message of the gospel.

Take divine revelation: if you say that Jesus Christ is the revelation of God, while as a matter of fact he is not God, then you have no way of claiming that what he says is really of God; there is then no fidelity between what he reveals and what God really is, and so the whole structure of divine revelation falls apart. In the second century Irenaeus had formulated the basic principle at stake as *God reveals himself through himself.* That was taken up by Karl Barth in our day, who, with the central point of the Nicene Creed in mind, expressed it thus: *the content of God's self-revelation is identical with Jesus Christ.* Sever that relation between Christ and God and revelation is emptied of any ultimate truth or reality, and you are then flung back upon a merely symbolical or mythological way of thinking and speaking. That is why the fathers at Nicaea held the unbroken relation in being and act between Jesus Christ the incarnate Son of God and God the Father to be absolutely central. They fought very hard for it, for in it the very gospel was at stake.

Or take the atonement, and this is a point that is today being discussed in a new way: if God became incarnate, then in some fundamental way GOD was at work in the cross. We do not of course believe like the heretic Praxeas in the crucifixion of the Father, but as Gregory Nazianzen pointed out, if salvation is an act of God himself, then we must really think of Jesus Christ as "God crucified." There are people today who talk a lot of nonsense about this in the so-called "God is dead" theology — an idea that did not emanate from Christian theology but from someone called Jean-Paul Richter, as well as Nietzsche and Hegel. "God is dead" is an utterly irrational idea. However, we are concerned in the gospel with a basic unity between the atoning sacrifice of Christ on the cross and the self-sacrifice of God the Father — there is an unbroken relation in being and act between them even at Calvary. But sever the ontological bond between them in Christ and the whole substance of the atonement is lost. That is what the ancient Catholic Church was up against in heretical denial of the deity of Jesus Christ, who for us and our salvation became man, when it inserted the clause on the oneness of the incarnated Son with the Father into the center of the Nicene Creed, in order to secure the saving truth of the cross of Christ and his atoning sacrifice.

Let me indicate the far-reaching significance of this by reference to *pastoral concern* today. I was a pastor of a church for ten years, during which I gained invaluable theological insights which I do not believe I could have got otherwise. I regret very much that many teachers and professors of theology in our colleges and seminaries, university faculties and departments of divinity today have had no pastoral experience. They are appointed to teach Christian theology and to train ministers of the gospel, but they themselves have very little personal experience in the actual ministry of the gospel. When I was a pastor I not only preached the gospel from the pulpit but I read the Scriptures and prayed with people in their homes regularly. When I had done that two or three times, they opened their hearts and talked frankly with me, which allowed me really to minister the gospel to them in a direct and personal way. It helped me to understand and preach the Word of God to them in a new personal way, which stood me in great stead later on when I was a professor of Christian dogmatics. Looking back I believe that I learned more in my two parishes about what goes on in the depths of human nature than I could ever have gained from psychological textbooks or college lectures.

During those years what imprinted itself upon my mind above all was the discovery of the deepest cry of the human heart: *Is God really like Jesus?* This came home to me very sharply one day on a battle field in Italy, when a fearfully wounded young lad, who was only nineteen and had but half an hour to live, said to me, "Padre, is God really like Jesus?" I assured him as he lay upon the ground with his life ebbing away that God is indeed really like Jesus, and that there is no unknown God behind the back of Jesus for us to fear; to see the Lord Jesus is to see the very face of God. When I thought about that afterwards, I asked myself, what has been happening, what has come in between Jesus Christ and God to obscure God from people? When

I went back to a parish in Aberdeen, an old lady who had not long to live said to me one day, "Dr. Torrance, is God really like Jesus?" — the very same words! You see, at the bottom of a person's heart, when the chips are down, when he or she is dying, but also at other times in life, the deep cry of the human heart for God is, *What is God really like?*"

Unfortunately, what the modern pursuit of so-called natural theology does is to drive a wedge between Jesus Christ and God, so that people come to think of God as some unknown terrifying deity behind the back of Jesus. That was what happened in the medieval world, as Calvin pointed out and as Barth has reiterated in our day: the division between natural theology and revealed theology had the effect of giving rise to a split in people's concept of God, as though knowledge of the one God is gained by reason while knowledge of the triune God is gained only by faith. That is why I could not agree with the dualism of Bernard Lonergan's two treatises, *De Deo Uno* and *De Deo Trino* — even Karl Rahner attacked that division in our knowledge of God rather sharply. It is only through Christ and in one Spirit that we have access to the Father and know God as one Being, three Persons. If we operate in theology with a split between Christ and God, that split is bound to enter into our knowledge of God himself — our concept of God becomes schizoid. Theological schizophrenia destroys human souls.

In preaching the Word of God and ministering the gospel to people, the most important thing with which we must be concerned is to bring them face-to-face with God in Jesus Christ, for it is only God in Jesus Christ who can forgive and heal — only God in Jesus Christ who can reveal the ultimate truth to us about himself. It is Jesus Christ alone who defines God for us, and defines him in a radical way that calls in question false notions of God arising out of alienation from him which obscure the truth and hide him from us. Today we need to learn again with the early Christians how, through faith in Jesus Christ as the one Mediator between God and humankind, to face and overcome the insidious effect of dualism, not only in our theology and science, but in our practical ministry, our pastoral care, our daily prayer, and our spiritual life.

Now let us consider further the emphasis in the early church upon the two main principles or doctrines I have been speaking about, which it formulated in terms of what was called the *homoousion* and the *hypostatic union*. The former refers to the oneness in being between Jesus Christ and God the Father, and the latter refers to the oneness in Christ between his divine and human natures. I do not believe that Christian theology since the early centuries has thought enough about this. If Jesus Christ is really of one and the same being as God the Father, then in a fundamental way the incarnation falls *within the life of God*. The incarnation therefore cannot be separated from the Holy Trinity. Now when we look at it in that way, the whole understanding of Christ, the Trinity, and divine revelation undergoes a sea change — we reach a dimension of depth in our grasp of the truth which we could not reach otherwise. But that dimension of depth has been missing in much of our theology. I have in mind here especially Western theology, Roman Catholic and Protestant theology alike, which suffers from serious flaws due to a persisting hangover of dualism from the ancient pagan world.

For many years I have been trying to show that in the doctrine of the Holy Trinity we discern the fundamental grammar of Christian theology. This is why I have been engaged with other Reformed church-men in theological dialogue with the Orthodox Church with a view to reaching a basic agreement in the doctrine of the Holy Trinity, in the hope that we may probe behind all the other traditional doctrines of the church and clear away or iron out our differences. I am glad to say that we have now reached and formulated an agreed statement on the doctrine of the Holy Trinity. This is an agreement which hinges upon the *homoousion,* the cardinal statement in the Nicene Creed, which enables us to grasp something of the oneness in being and act between what God is toward us and for us in the gospel as Father, Son, and Holy Spirit, and what he is antecedently and eternally in himself. We believe that the formulation of this doctrinal agreement on the Holy Trinity is of far-reaching ecumenical significance, for it helps to under-mine historical differences between the East and the West. This applies, not least, to disagreements over the central doctrine of Christ as the incarnate Son of God, the one Mediator between God and humankind, apart from whom there is no salvation. But it also points ahead to a deeper and more unified grasp of the Eucharist.

This brings us to the other main principle formulated by the church fathers, known as the *hypostatic union*. The hypostatic union means that in Jesus Christ, God and man, divine and human nature, are indissolubly united in one incarnate person, so that the whole of Christ's life from beginning to end was a life lived in unbroken relation with God the Father. In that event the saving work of Christ and his incarnate life are inseparable. Redemption begins with the very advent of Jesus, so that his conception and birth of the Virgin Mary are to be regarded as essential constituents in his saving activity, and his humanity is seen to be not just a means to an end. Atoning reconciliation is to be understood as taking place within the incarnate constitution of the Mediator. His person and his work are one. That is why the New Testament can say that Jesus Christ *is* redemption, he *is* righteousness, he *is* life eternal. He himself in his incarnate person *is* our salvation. This means that we have to understand the incarnation and the atonement in terms of their internal relations within the incarnate constitution of Christ as God and man.

If this is the case we must not flinch from the statement of St. Paul in the Epistle to the Romans (8:3) that the Son of God came among us in the concrete likeness of sinful flesh (ἐν ὁμοιώματι σαρκὸς ἁμαρτίας — cf. Phil. 2:7: ἐν ὁμοιώματι ἀνθρώπων), yet far from sinning himself he condemned sin in the flesh. Nor must we try to water down St. Paul's statement that Christ was made sin for us, although he knew no sin (2 Cor. 5:21). That is to say, in becoming man the Son of God became one of us and one with us as we actually are, thereby making our sin and our death his own so that he might really take our place and redeem us from them. This was a point of crucial significance for theologians like Irenaeus, Gregory Nazianzen, and Cyril of Alexandria, who used to point out that what Christ has not taken up from us is unhealed, what he has not assumed is not saved. Many people in the West have found this soteriological principle rather difficult and have preferred to think of Christ as having taken upon himself human nature as it came from the hand of God before the fall, but that is to separate the incarnation from reconciliation, the person of Christ from his saving work. Was Jesus not the Savior of the Virgin Mary, as she claimed?

I believe that it is very crucial for us to hold this truth, that the Savior took our fallen Adamic humanity upon him, but we must add that in the very act of taking it he was at work redeeming and sanctifying it in himself, which he continued to do throughout the whole of his sinless earthly life. Hence we must think of his incarnating and atoning activities as interpenetrating one another from the very beginning to the end of his oneness with us. Otherwise the humanity of Christ has to be thought of only in an instrumentalist way, and the atonement can be formulated only in terms of external moral relations or legal transactions. But if the incarnation is itself essentially redemptive and not just a means to an end, then atonement must be regarded as taking place in the ontological depths of Christ's incarnate life, in which he penetrated into the very bottom of our fallen human being and took our disobedient humanity, even our alienated human mind, upon himself in order to heal it and convert it back in himself into union with God. Indeed, he even penetrated into and took our original sin upon himself in order to redeem us from it by bringing his atoning sacrifice and holiness to bear upon it in the very roots of our human existence and being. The hypostatic union and the atoning union imply one another and are the obverse of one another.

What happened to the notion of atonement in the West? Throughout the history of the church and its theology, with few exceptions like John McLeod Campbell, H. R. Mackintosh, and Karl Barth, the atonement and the incarnation have not really been thought into one another, so that the doctrine of atonement has usually been expounded in terms of the external relations of the moral order that has not yet been redeemed, and in terms of a legal order that has not yet come under the saving and renewing work of Christ. This seems to me to be one of the most disastrous things that has happened in the history of the church, for it has led to a one-sided forensic or legalistic understanding of the saving work of Christ in which much of its profound truth and beauty has been distorted. Think, for example, of what happened under the imperious development of canon law in the West. When the church proclaimed the gospel in the early centuries it did not evangelize the foundations of Roman law, either in Byzantium or in Rome, so that Christian dogmas were steadily given canonical formulation by church lawyers in terms of existing law, which, although it was doubtless somewhat adapted to decisions of the church, was not really evangelized or Christianized. Think of the problems this presented to people like St. Thomas Aquinas, who found himself constrained to express his understanding of evangelical truths within canonical structures already laid down in the *codex iuris canonici*. Read St. Thomas's *Commentary on the Four Gospels* and compare his teaching there with his formalization of doctrines in the *Summa Theologica*. Much the same thing happened in Protestant, and particularly in Calvinist and Lutheran, theology, not least over the doctrine of atonement, which is regularly expounded within the frame of external moral and judicial relations instead of within the frame of God's relation to the world established by the incarnation of his Son in Jesus Christ. That is really the result of allowing dualism to eat into the very heart of the Christian faith at this most sensitive point, in atonement, where incarnation and atonement are separated from one another or are only superficially related to one another. In the teaching of the New Testament, it is the Father-Son relation that constitutes the unifying frame within which all Christian doctrines, but also all Christian understanding of the world, are shaped. I have in mind here particularly the doctrine of the atonement. But, alas, that is very different from what happened to the doctrine of the atonement in the formularies of Roman, Lutheran, and Calvinist orthodoxy.

The Incarnation and Atonement in the Light of Our Scientific Understanding of the World God Has Created

Let us look again at what happened when the *homoousion* was formulated in the early church, when it was stressed that Jesus Christ is of one being with the Father: it had the effect of destroying the place of Greek dualism in theology and of calling for a reconstruction of the foundations of knowledge. Hence the basic terms and concepts used by the fathers in theological formulation, even if they were taken over from Greek thought, cannot be interpreted except as they were transformed and radically altered under the impact of the gospel. I believe that something similar has to happen in our thinking today — we must allow the unity of God and man in Christ, and the inner relation of creation and redemption brought about through the incarnation, to overcome the dualism still latent in the patterns of thought that we have inherited from the past and that are still deeply embedded in our culture, so that we may think out with appropriateness and rigor God's saving interaction with us in space and time. I have already pointed out that in the early church theologians had to destroy epistemological and cosmological dualism in order to make room for the gospel and to develop in a more profound ontological and epistemological way a realist understanding of God's revealing and saving acts in history. But in the modern world that dualism has already been destroyed, largely through general relativity theory in its unification of geometry and physics, which had a profound effect on the logical structure of science in the integration of theoretical and empirical factors in knowledge at every level of inquiry and experience. The transformation this brought about in the general scientific outlook of today enables us to proclaim the gospel and teach the truth of Christ within the structure and concepts of space and time, which the early church could not do without immense struggle.

I would now like to focus attention on several points in regard to which dialogue between theology and science is particularly significant for us today.

(1) The universe of space and time as understood by the new science is far more congenial to Christian theology than that developed by ancient science or by Enlightenment science.

Several years ago I was asked to write a "critique" of Pope John Paul II's "Message on Science and Religion" when the Vatican Observatory was commemorating the third centenary of the publication of Newton's *Principia Mathematica*. I first wrote one which the authorities turned down, for in it I suggested that the Pope's message appeared to have suffered from the attention of the Curia! Then I wrote another one which they accepted. This time I took my cue from the counsel offered by the Pope in pointing to the achievement of the medieval masters in the difficult task of relating theology and science, compared to modern science, which he seemed to think challenged the Christian faith "far more deeply." I pointed out with reference to St. Thomas Aquinas that the synthesis worked out in the thirteenth century between theology and science was between Christian theology and pagan science, whereas the kind of science that stems from the seventeenth century and the new science of our own times has definitely Judeo-Christian foundations, and that the latter is much more congenial to Christianity.

I believe firmly that this is the case. On the one hand, I have found the thought of great scientists like James Clerk Maxwell, Albert Einstein, and Michael Polanyi to be helpful in my theological activity. But on the other hand, I have found that when you try to expound the truth of the gospel in a rigorous scientific way, you meet with a reaction from scientists that is sometimes rather overwhelming. I will never forget, for example, that when I published *Space, Time and Incarnation,* I received a letter from Professor Alan Cook (now Sir Alan Cook), a very distinguished scientist who was later to be head of the Cavendish Laboratories in Cambridge, who told me how much he appreciated and agreed with what I had written, and recommended me to make more use of general relativity! What astonished me was that here was a scientist reacting to an unashamed account of the incarnation in space and time and finding it helpful. I meet with a similar reaction again and again today, which indicates that there is a two-way traffic in ideas between theology and science which is rather more positive and helpful than many theologians think.

I find it rather sad that many theologians and biblical scholars today are frightened of having conceptual contact with scientists. Is not the reason for this that they are still tied to an obsolete notion of science as rigidly causalist and determinist, which leaves no room for God's interaction with our space-time world, or therefore for divine revelation, incarnation, atonement, or resurrection? Theologians and biblical scholars like these need to come into the modern world and engage in conceptual interchange with scientists, which cannot but prove helpful. Of course, this may also have the effect of exposing some of the pseudo-scientific ideas lurking in their epistemological assumptions, but along with that cleansing process they will find dialogue with the new science a greater aid than they may imagine in their own particular academic disciplines.

(2) The recent appreciation by science of singularity is very encouraging for the church's witness to the uniqueness of Christ.

The concept of singularity was abhorrent to classical modern science, for in the Enlightenment a way of thinking became dominant in philosophy and science in which singularities had no place. In order to engage in rational or scientific processes of thought, one had to resolve away all particulars in order to arrive at what is universally, timelessly, and necessarily true. That is what Newton did, following the ancient Greek and medieval habit of thinking in terms of universals, in accordance with the classical paradigm of geometry — that is why, for example, in the *Principia Mathematica* Newton sought to give expression to all scientific knowledge within the frame of the necessary timeless relations of Euclidean geometry. That was a procedure destroyed by Einstein in his integration of geometry and experience, which convinced him that if mathematical propositions are logically and timelessly certain they are just not true, and that if they are true, that is, really consonant with nature, they are not certain, which had the effect of changing the basic concept of natural or physical law. Today, however, the classical way of resolving away all particularities in the formulation of comprehensive physical laws has been shattered also by discovery of the "black hole" (as John Wheeler called it), the original dense state of all matter and energy in the universe, which is an absolute singularity.

More significant than the "black hole" for Christian theology, I believe, is the place which the unique role of *light* and its invariant speed have come to occupy in our understanding of the universe and its open-structured laws. Thus, as Hermann Weyl once expressed it, *light has a unique metaphysical status in the universe,* for while all motion is defined relationally in terms of space and time, and space and time are defined relationally in terms of light, light is not defined with reference to anything else. It is upon the invariance or constancy of the speed of light that all order in the empirical universe finally depends — if the speed of light were to vary, there would be universal disorder.

I believe that God has created the universe in such a way that the invariance of light in its creaturely way is a reflection of his eternal invariance, his unchangeableness, and his faithfulness. If light were to wobble, the universe would be thrown into complete lawlessness. If God were to wobble, if God were not to be utterly faithful, the same yesterday, today, and forever, there would be an utterly chaotic state of affairs in all space and time. It is with reference to this correlation between the absolute uniqueness of God and the created uniqueness of light that we may give firm expression to theological truths in a form that people in our modern scientific world can appreciate.

Let us return, then, to the concept of *singularity,* which helps many people today to appreciate in a new way the biblical teaching about the uniqueness and once-for-all-ness of the incarnation of the Son of God in Jesus Christ, the way, the truth, and the life, apart from whom there is no way to know God. There is only one Christ, and there could only be one who is God and man in one person. The singularity, the transcendence, and the finality of Christ are today everywhere being denied and rejected in the so-called multi-faith culture, in which there is no room for the singularity of God's self-revelation in Jesus Christ; but this involves on the part of many theologians and biblical scholars a tragic lapse back into the rationalistic relativism of the Enlightenment, which ruled out of court any academic or scientific study of Christianity, unless Christianity is treated as only one religion in a universal class of religions. Today, however, scientists are beginning to take the singularity of the incarnation and of Christ

seriously, and they now have less difficulty in appreciating and understanding the uniqueness and transcendence of the Lord Jesus Christ,
in contrast to the backward thinking of theological teachers and biblical
scholars in the widespread movement to replace theological faculties
with departments of religious studies.

*(3) The oneness in God of his being and his act, already
adumbrated in patristic theology, calls for a new way of thinking.*

If God and man are indissolubly united in the one person of Jesus
Christ, that must be understood with reference back to an ultimate
ground in the very nature of God. If what God is toward us and for
us in the incarnation and atonement he is eternally and inherently in
himself, if the activity of God in the economic Trinity is identical with
the activity of God in the immanent Trinity, then the being of God
must be understood not in a static but in a *dynamic* way. This was the
point which Athanasius drove home in his stress upon ἐνούσιος ἐνέρ-
γεια (together with ἐνούσιος λόγος), the *activity inherent in the very
being of God.* That is admittedly a totally un-Greek conception, which
could not but import a decisive change in the foundations of thought.
Consider the significance of this in the light of our modern scientific
rejection of dualism; it implies a fundamental way of thinking which
is at once *dynamical and ontological,* which is what modern science has
been struggling to achieve in its attempts to harmonize relativity theory
and quantum theory.

Difficult problems arise here in connection with the spatial and
temporal aspects of nature thrown into prominence by the discovery
that light is found to behave both as a particle and as a wave, which is
only partially solved by the finding that light particles or photons can
be understood as packets of waves. In his dissatisfaction with the relic
of dualism that this still implied, Einstein wanted to go further in a
realist development of a fully relativistic quantum theory, and certainly
physics has moved and is still moving in that direction. However, it
does not seem possible to eradicate completely the distinction between

particle and wave, any more than it would be possible to do away with the difference between the spatial and temporal aspects of nature. Nevertheless there is clearly a pervasive unity in the behavior of nature, which calls for ways of thinking in which *ontological and dynamic factors* are construed together, although we are unable to do that with the conceptual instruments we now have. This means that we have to develop new conceptual instruments with which to grasp and express the subtle, refined behavior found in the dynamic and contingent structures of the universe.

Is this way of thinking not only one which the ancient church anticipated but one with which theologians must still be concerned if they are to be faithful to God's revealing and saving acts in the incarnation and atonement? Let me refer again to my old teacher Karl Barth, because this is precisely what he actually did in bringing together the patristic emphasis upon the being of God in his acts and the Reformation emphasis upon the acts of God in his being. The relation between the being of God and his acts had fallen foul of medieval-Aristotelian dualism and the inertial notion of deity that went with it, so that understanding of the being and of the acts of God became separated in theology. Similarly the Reformation emphasis upon the mighty acts of God, particularly evident in its stress upon redemption, fell foul of Newtonian and Enlightenment dualism and the deistic notion of God that went with it, so that ontology tended to drop out of Protestant theology. This is very evident in the regular disjunction between incarnation and atonement, but where more than in the application to biblical interpretation of the absurd idea of *zeitlose Ereignisse* or timeless events?

It is to the great merit of Karl Barth, however, that with a herculean effort of thought he brought both the patristic and the Reformation ways of thinking together in his doctrine of the being of God in his acts and the acts of God in his being. The section of his *Church Dogmatics* 2.1 in which he set out that doctrine (one which I was privileged to hear as lectures) is probably one of the greatest works of Christian theology ever written. His teaching there about the nature of God had certainly been anticipated by Athanasius, but it had never been worked out in the tremendous form it was given by Barth in a profound integration of the ontological and dynamic ingredients in divine revelation and Christian theology. Doubtless it is that combination of the ontological and the dynamic that makes Barth's *Church Dogmatics* so difficult for people who are still tied to dualist, static, and analytical ways of thinking. On the other hand, when we learn to combine ontological and dynamic modes of thought, I believe we can make remarkable contact with our scientist friends, who sometimes tell us that with Karl Barth theological science had already done forty years ago what they are still trying to achieve in physics.

(4) The bearing of the doctrine of the Trinity upon knowledge of God in his internal relations.

In the second chapter of the Epistle to the Ephesians St. Paul insists that authentic knowledge of God derives from God's revelation of himself within Israel, and that apart from Israel Gentiles are without God and without hope, for the oracles, the covenant, and the promises of God all belong to Israel. On the other hand, he also insists that it is only through the cross of Christ that we are reconciled to God and that the barrier between us and God is broken down, that we may really know God, as through the Son and the Spirit we are given access to the Father. It is only through incarnation and atonement, through Christ and the Spirit, that knowledge of God as he is in himself is opened to us. Really to know God is to know him, not in an undifferentiated oneness of his being, but in his internal differentiations or relations as the Father, the Son, and the Holy Spirit, and thus as the Holy Trinity, "One Being, three Persons," Μία Οὐσία, Τρεῖς Ὑποστάσεις, as it was expressed in classical patristic theology.

This trinitarian understanding of God is a point I sometimes discuss with my Jewish friends. I point out to them that it is Jews who above all have destroyed the Kantian notion that we do not know things in themselves but only as they appear to us. That is to say, they have taught us that we really know things when we know things in their internal relations. In that case, I ask them why they do not apply that to knowledge of God, instead of being content with some rather negative Kantian-like borderline notion of God empty of internal content. Is that not what happens, I ask, when they think of God as an undifferentiated oneness, for no one can have a conceptual grasp of God unless in some sense he or she knows him in his internal relations? I recall the point made by Spinoza that God loves himself so that there are *relations of love within God.* This is how Martin Buber himself spoke of the possibility of having a *conceptual grasp of God,* in rejecting a merely negative borderline notion of God. Thus it turns out that on both scientific and theological grounds it now becomes possible for Christians to speak with Jews about differentiations in knowledge of the one being of God. Even at this point of wide divergence radical science is breaking down the barriers that have been erected in history, not only between Jews and Gentiles, but between Christians and believing Jews. It does mean, however, that we must work out together the far-reaching epistemological consequences of the rejection of dualist ways of thought for theological as well for natural science. It is the doctrine of the Holy Trinity that can play a decisive role here.

(5) The question of time and atonement.

This was also a subject raised in the early church. If we believe that in Jesus Christ the Creator Word by whom all things were made and in whom all things hold together became man within space and time, then we cannot but think with St. Paul of the incarnate and atoning action of God in Christ as penetrating back in time to the very beginning, gathering it up in himself, and thrusting forward in time to the very end in the consummation of his creative and redemptive purpose. We have to do here with *real time* (to borrow an expression from Henri Bergson), not with a Platonic notion of time as a moving image of eternity. This realist understanding of the incarnation as the redemptive recapitulation of all time since the creation and as the teleological fulfillment of time was a favorite conception of Irenaeus in the second century, and through him it was injected into the classical theology of the early church. This carries with it a concept of the *redemption of time*, which challenges us today to work out a deeper conception of time in the light of the radical change brought about through the incarnation and the atonement, and then in the light of a feedback from this change to reach a fuller appreciation of God's activity in incarnation and atonement.

Important questions about the relation of God to time are inevitably raised here. One of the most significant was highlighted by Athanasius when he pointed out that while God was always Father he was not always Creator — there was a "time" when God was not Creator. This implies that when God created the world out of nothing we must think of that as something completely new, *new even for God!* In seeking to understand that, Athanasius went to the incarnation: the Son of God was not always incarnate, which meant that the incarnation also was something *new even for God*. In this event we must think of there being a "before" and an "after" in the life of God. We cannot really grasp what that means, but it does imply that somehow "time" characterizes the life of God. We distinguish between the uncreated light of God and created light, between the uncreated life of God and created life, just as we distinguish between uncreated being and created being. Similarly I believe we must think of uncreated time as well as created time. This is a distinction the depth of which we cannot fathom, but while we cannot understand what uncreated time is, we can be sure that God gathers up our creaturely time, even fallen time, and embraces it redemptively within the uncreated time of his eternal life.

In our day the nature of time has been brought into the very center of scientific inquiry, particularly in connection with entropy and thermodynamics and the establishment, in departure from Newtonian concepts formulated in reversible equations, of the irreversibility or arrow of time. I have in mind here particularly the work of Peter Landsberg and Ilya Prigogine and the notion of time as intrinsic to objects, which implies with it a conception that the future is open and not deterministically closed. In such an open universe *time is redeemable*. Thus in his account of non-equilibrium thermodynamics or the thermodynamics of open systems, in which real time has to do with the world of becoming, Prigogine does not hesitate to speak of *the redemption of time*. Here again in a very difficult area we find a careful scientific way of thinking which is fundamentally congenial to the Christian faith. Whatever the redemption of time may mean in a conception of the openness and continuous expansion of the universe, it does confront Christian theology with a challenge to think out some very important issues in a new way. If the incarnation and atonement involve a penetration not only back in time but also forward in time, then all time has to be understood under God as slanted toward the future. In this case theologians must surely be obliged to work out, however tentatively, some kind of relation between eschatology and cosmology. That is undoubtedly a difficult task, and it is one which we may attempt only if we take seriously the notion of the redemption of time and the final renewal of heaven and earth in Christ the incarnate Word of God, who is the Last as well as the First, the Omega as well as the Alpha of all God's ways and works.

Let me recall at this point that the New Testament speaks of the advent of Christ as *parousia* / παρουσία — the coming which is a presence and the presence which is a coming. It never uses the term in the plural but only in the singular, for there is only one *parousia* which reaches from the birth of Jesus in our space-time world to his coming again at the consummation of history. We live in the midst of that one *parousia,* ἐν τῷ μεταξὺ τῆς παρουσίας αὐτοῦ χρόνῳ, as Justin Martyr expressed it in the second century. If that is so, there is an "eschatological moment" that spans our life here and now risen with Christ and our resurrection in the body when Christ comes again. How can we understand that? I think in this connection of what Einstein called the "relativity of simultaneity," according to which it is possible for one event in the physical world to have two different "real times." That helps us to understand something of the teaching of the Epistle to the Ephesians, which refers in the aorist tense to our being risen with Christ as having already taken place, and yet we still wait for our resurrection in the body to take place at the return of Christ. It is that dynamic way of thinking which brings together what has happened once and for all and what is yet to take place without in any way detracting from real time that baffles people. In much the same way, some people find it difficult to follow Karl Barth when he brings together ontological and dynamic factors in his account of salvation and faith, the once for all and the still to come. That is due, I think, to a dualist hangover in their understanding of incarnation and atonement, and the redemption of time which it involves.

In drawing this address to a close I would like to return to the question I have been trying to answer in connection with my membership in two international academies devoted to theology and to science. It is the question whether there is a way of bringing scientists and theologians together in which rigorous science and rigorous theology can enter into a serious dialogue with one another without betrayal of their respective convictions. While we do not and may not try to build theology on science, any more than we build science on theology, there is nevertheless a deep level of conceptual interconnection between the two, clarification of which can help both theology and science to be faithful to the distinctive nature of the realities with which they are concerned. Dialogue with one another within the overlap of their inquiries in space and time may help scientists to shed dubious theological ideas that they may have unwittingly picked up in the history of thought, and may help theologians to shed discarded scientific ideas which they also may have picked up from the past. Hence, rightly pursued, this kind of dialogue involves a process of mutual purification and increasing rapprochement. When we theologians engage in it in this way we become better equipped to preach the gospel of the incarnation and atonement in the scientific world in which we live today.